TURKEY

PHOTOGRAPHS BY ELIZABETH KRAMER

THIS IS PART OF THE VISITING SERIES.

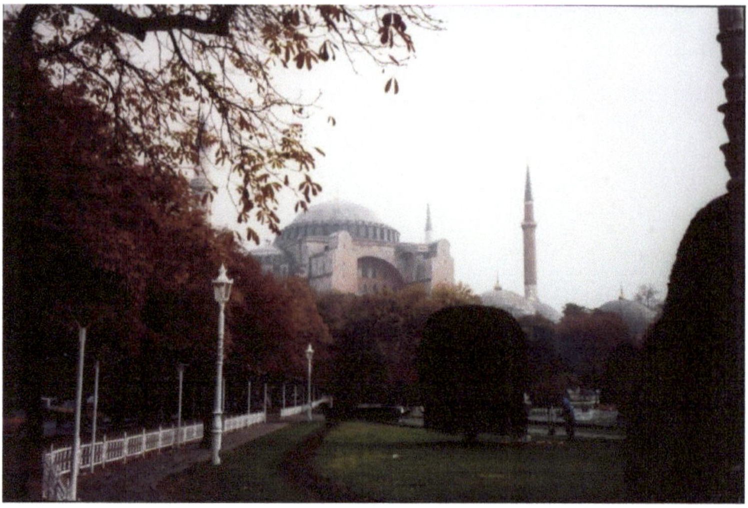

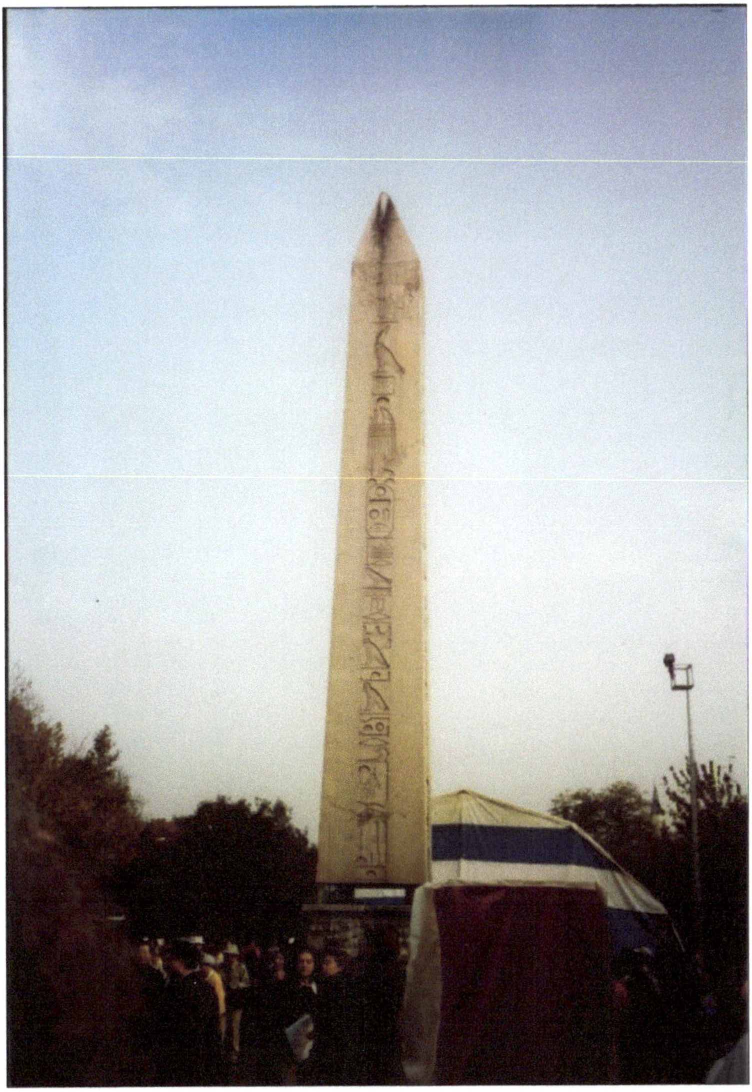

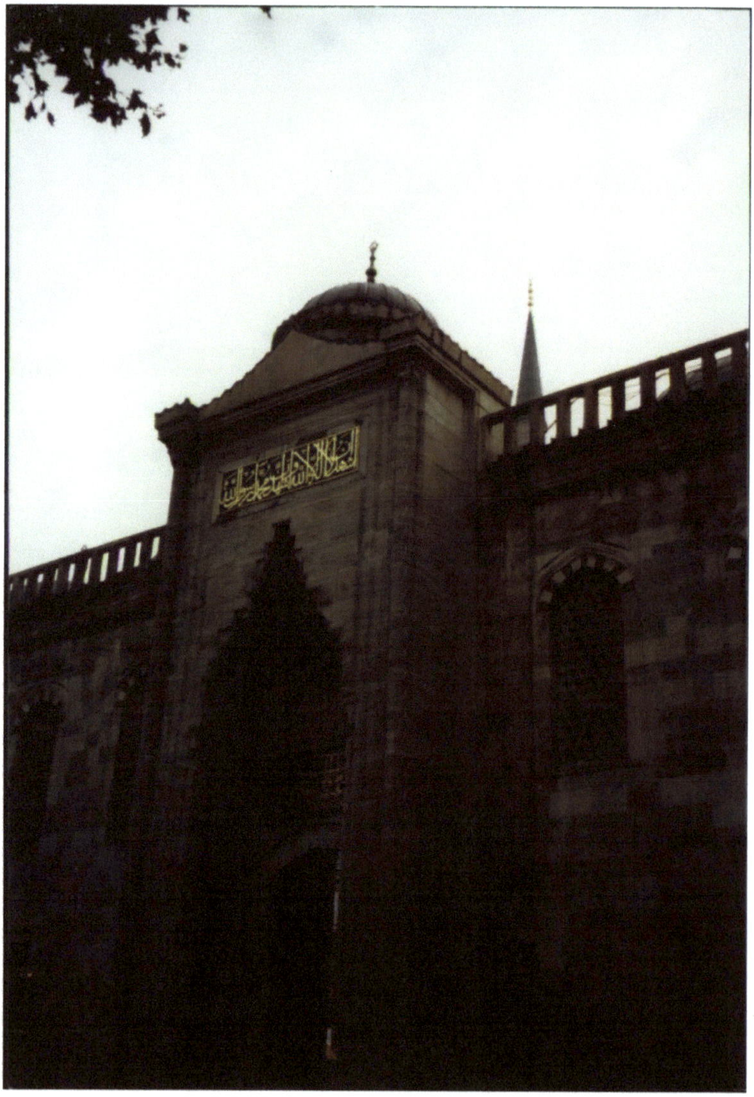

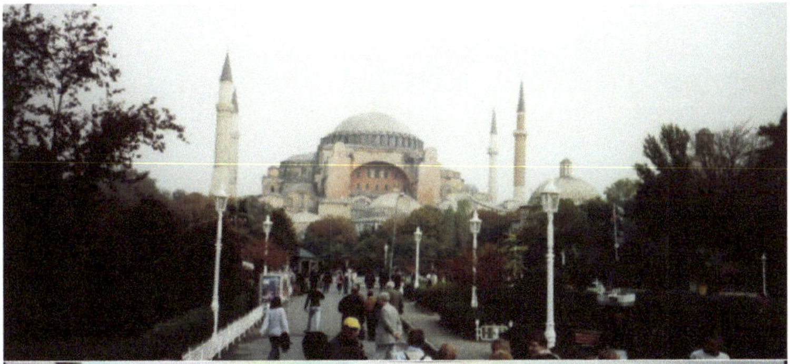

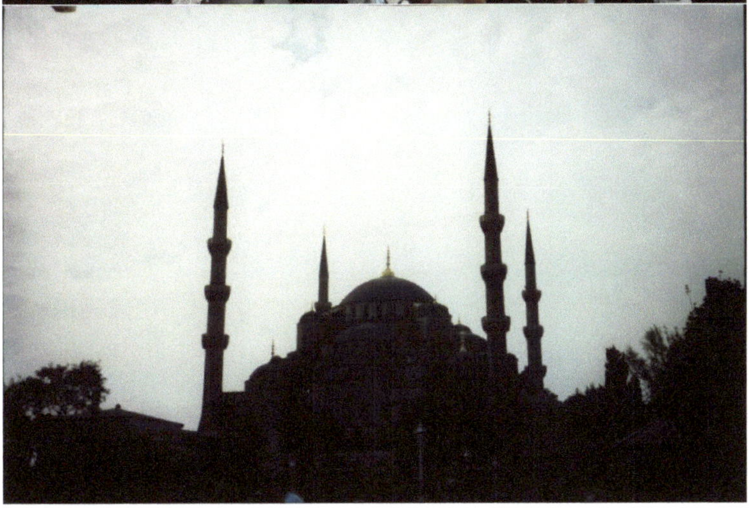

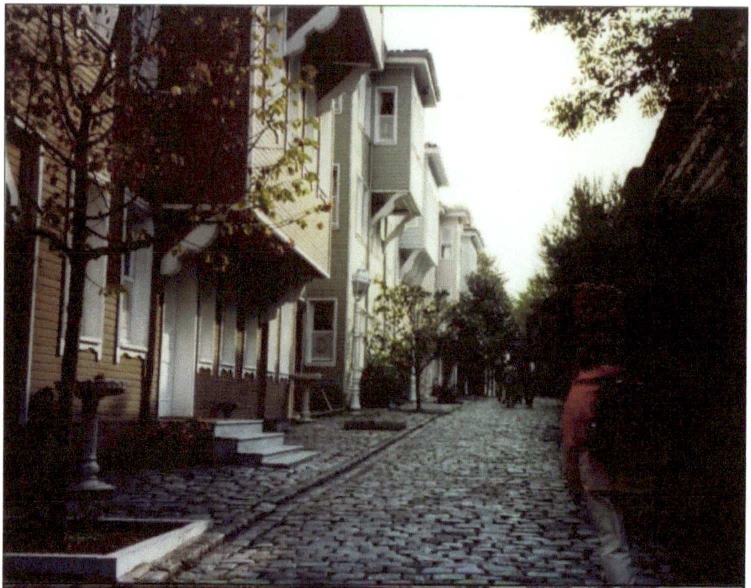

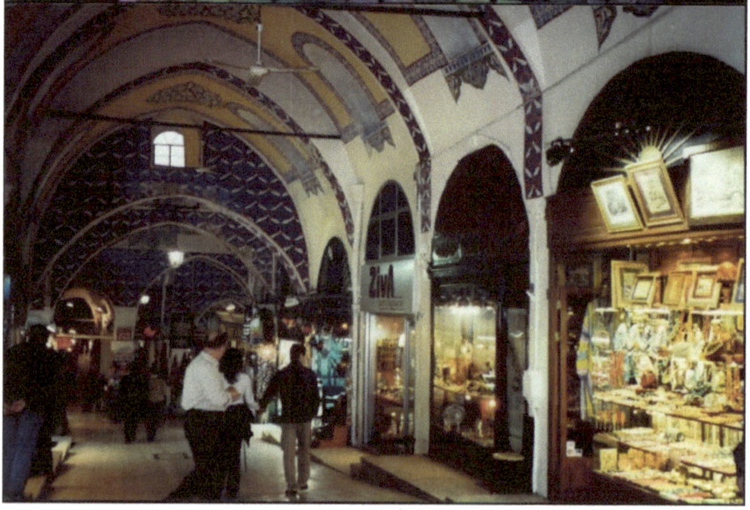

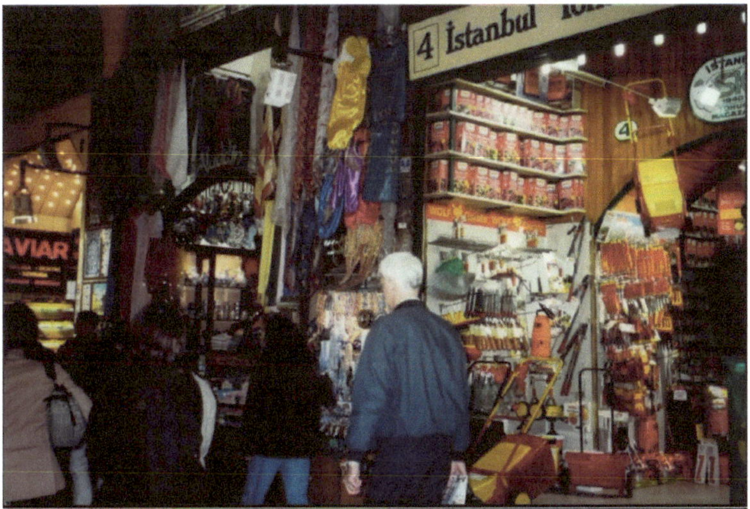
4 İstanbul

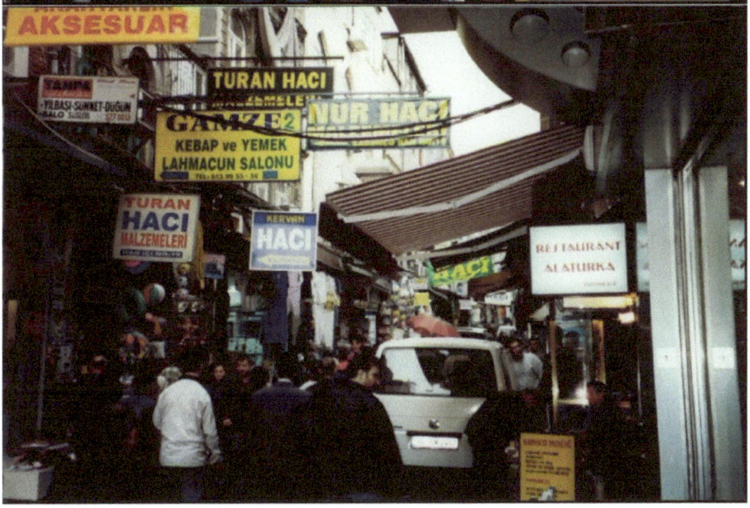
AKSESUAR
TURAN HACI
GAMZE 2
KEBAP ve YEMEK
LAHMACUN SALONU
NUR HACI
TURAN
HACI
MALZEMELERİ
KERVAN
HACI
RESTAURANT
ALATURKA

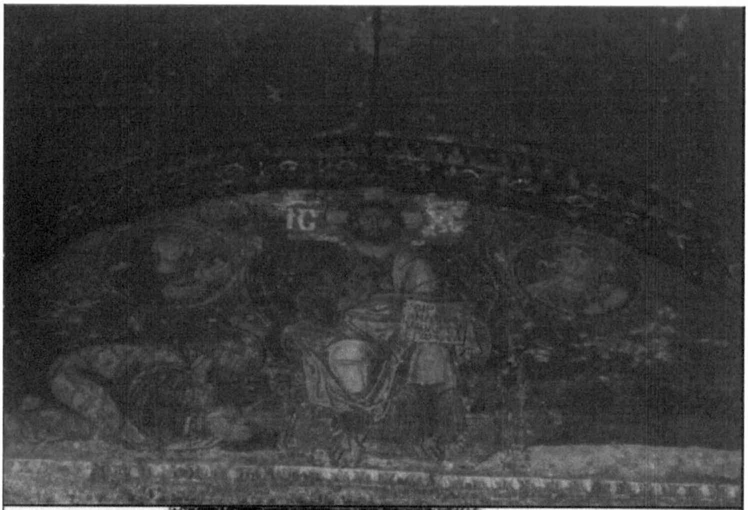
IC

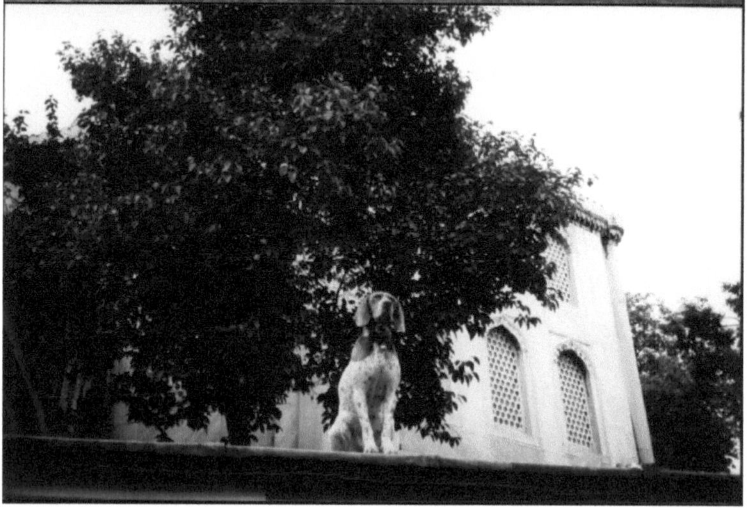

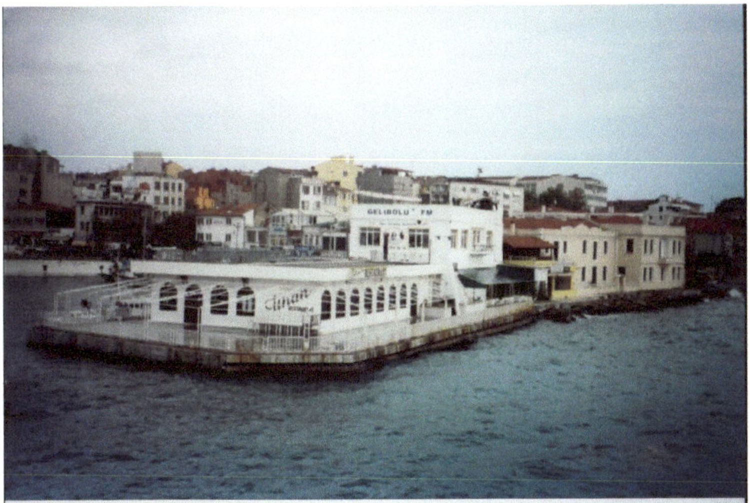
GELIBOLU FM

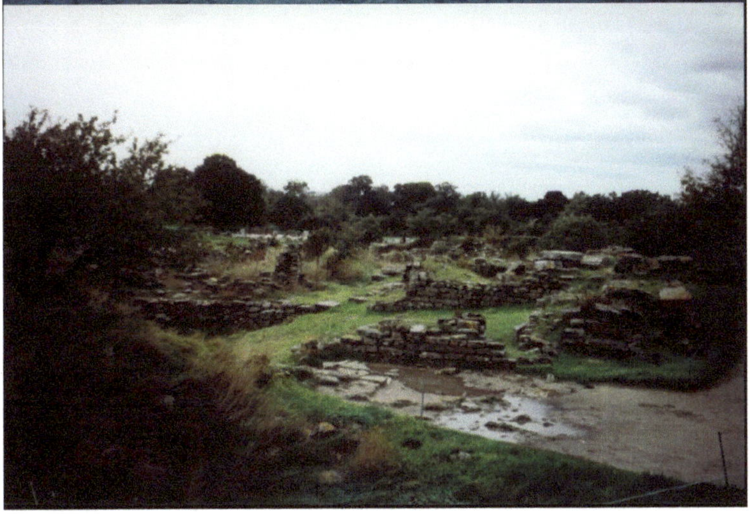

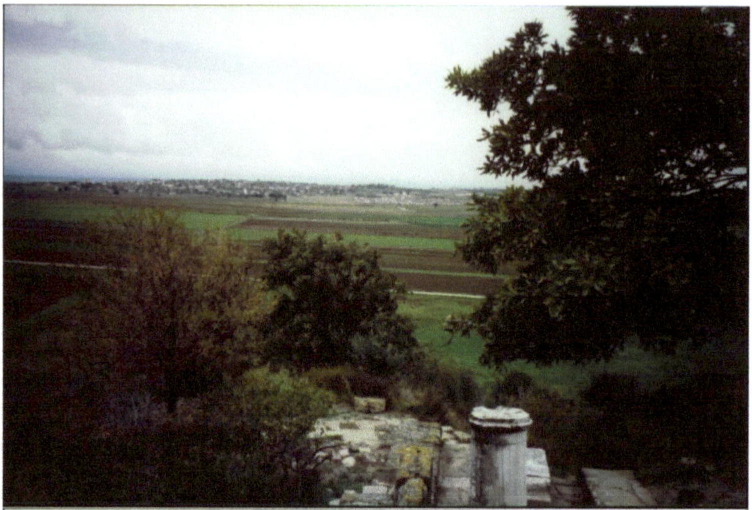

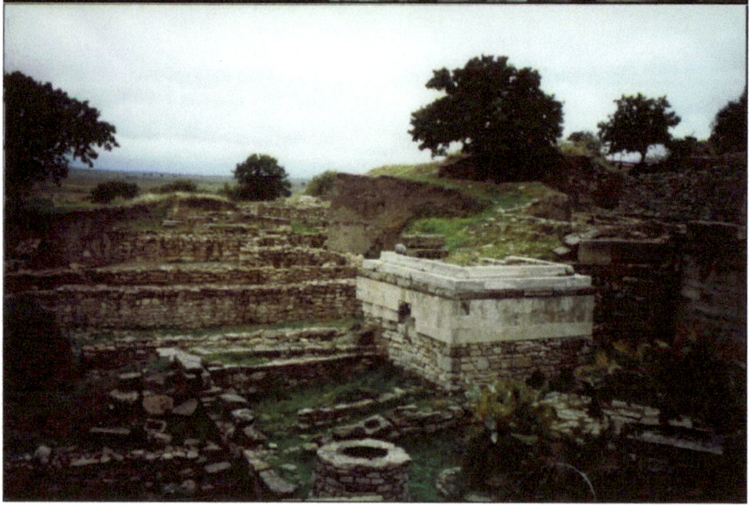

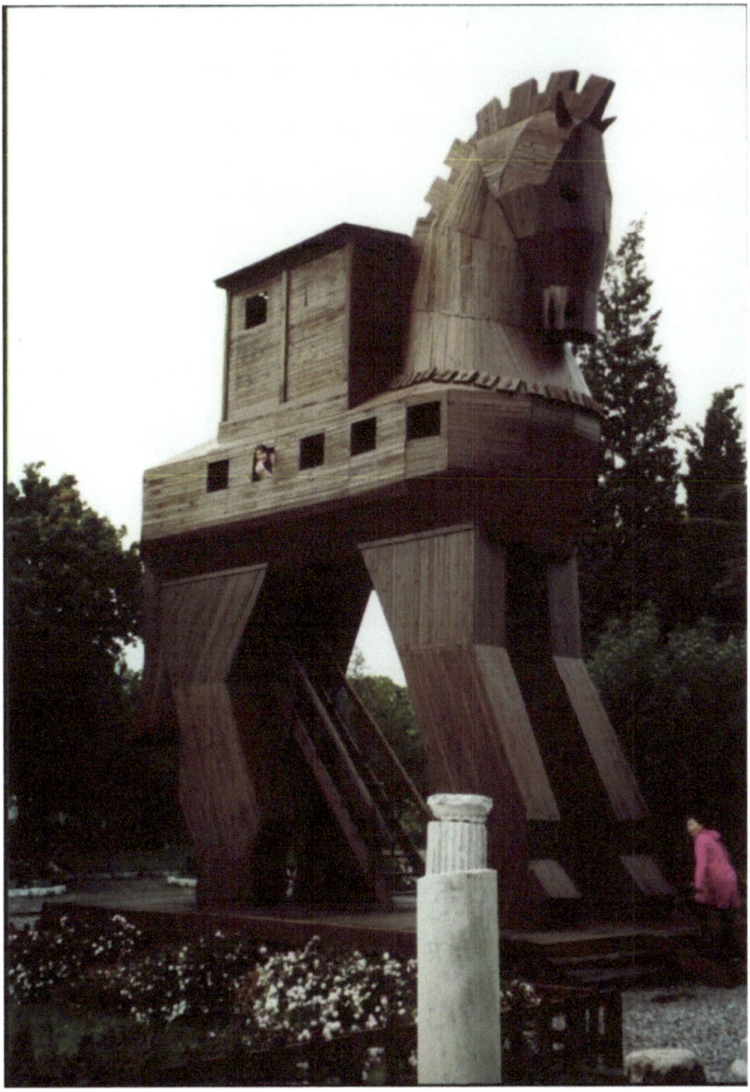

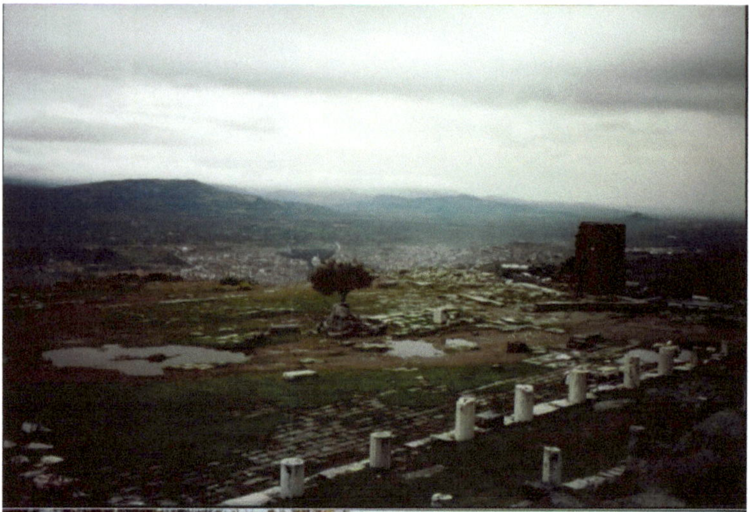
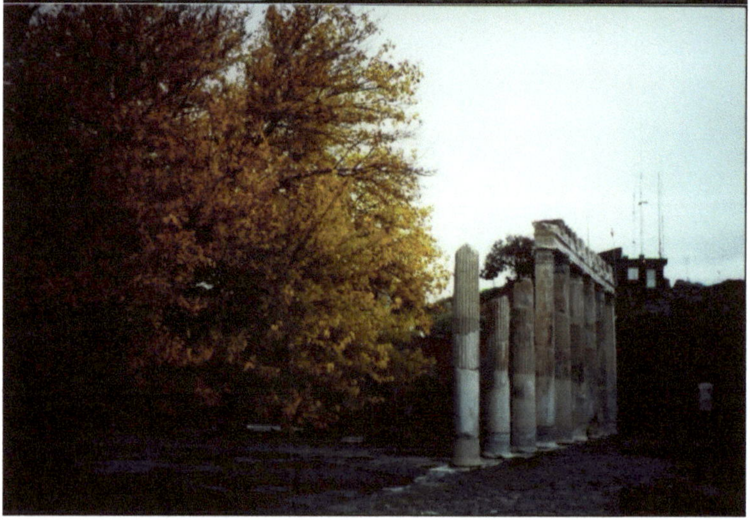

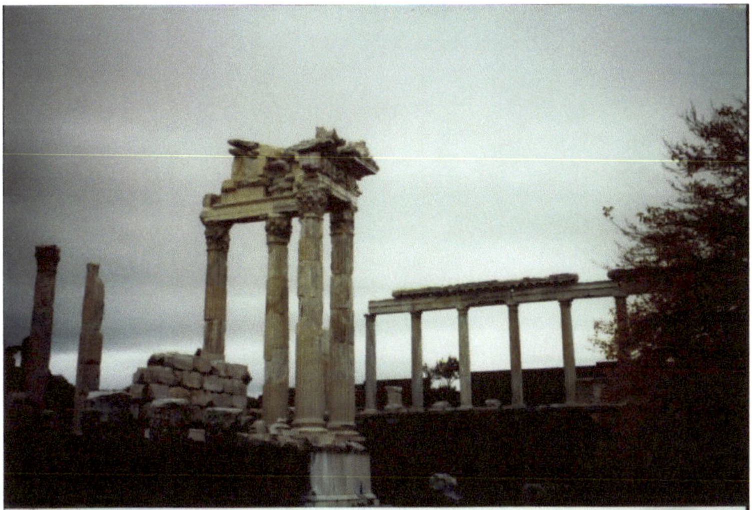

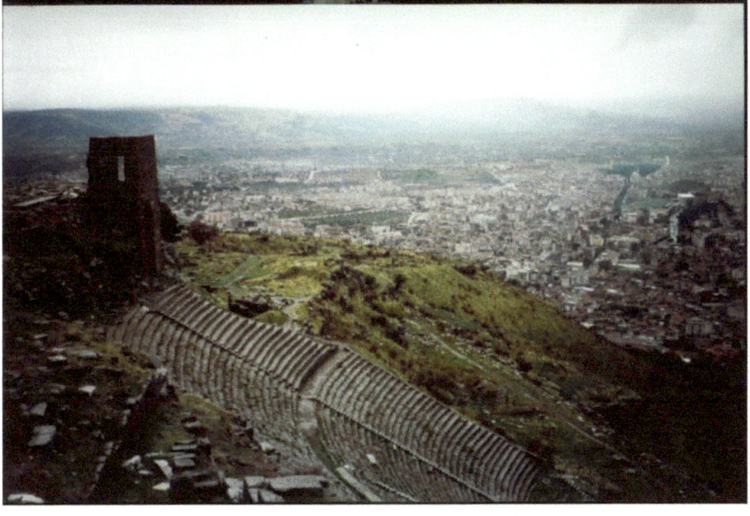

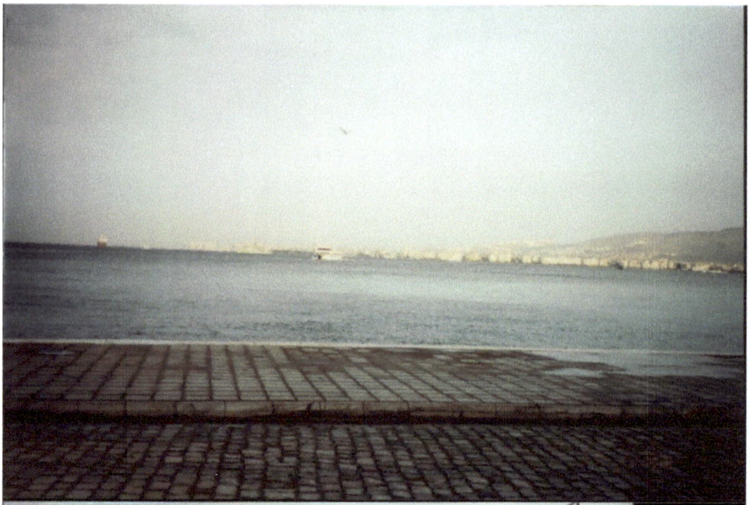

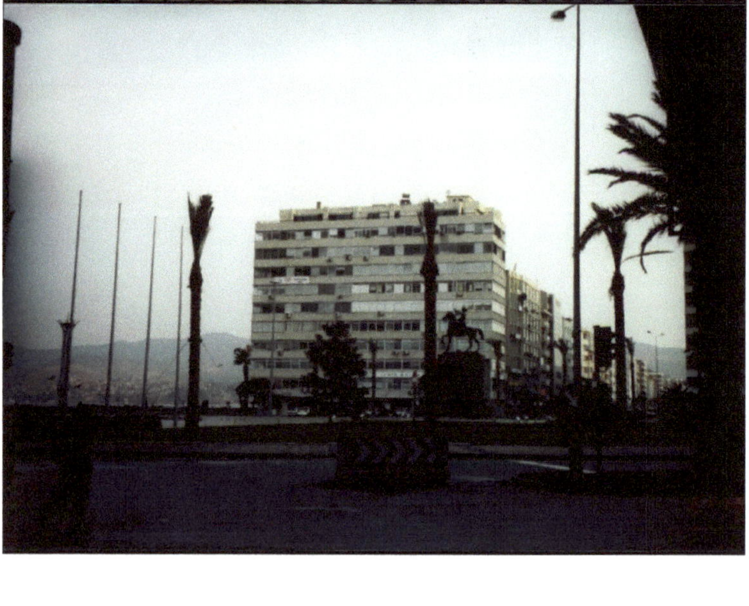

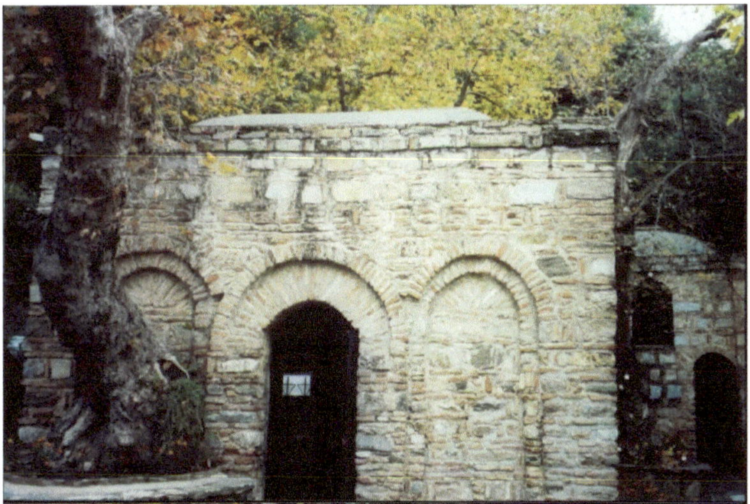

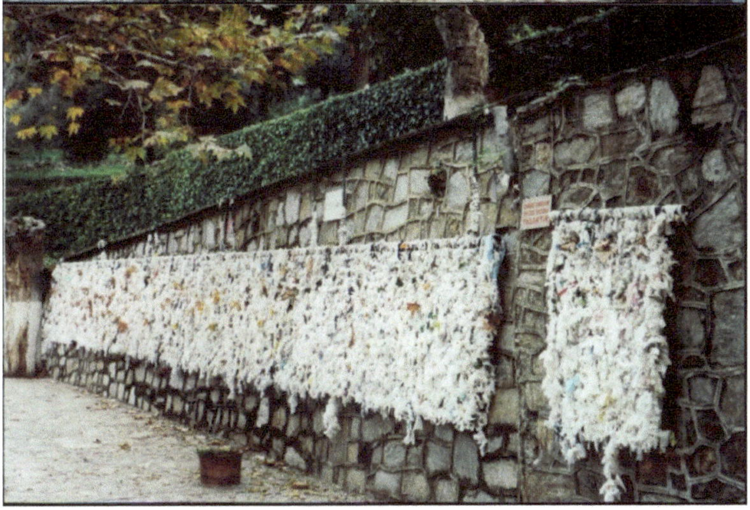

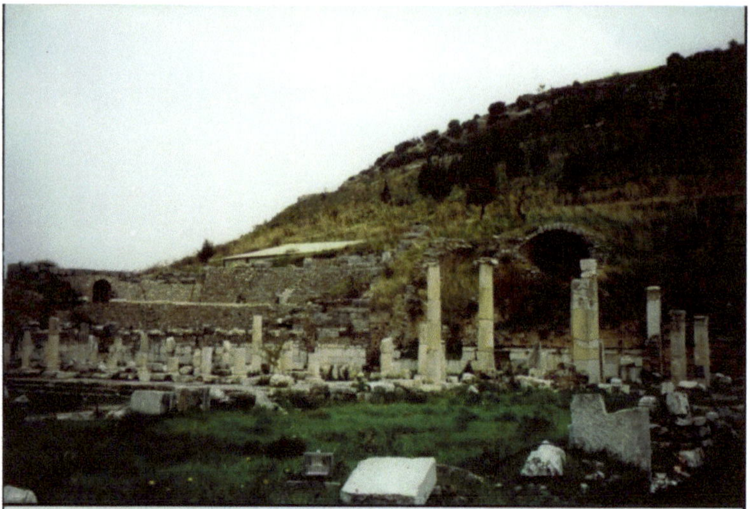

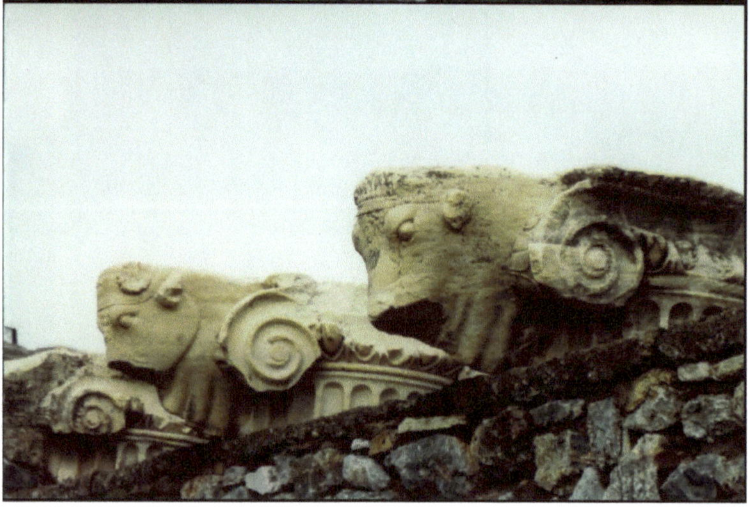

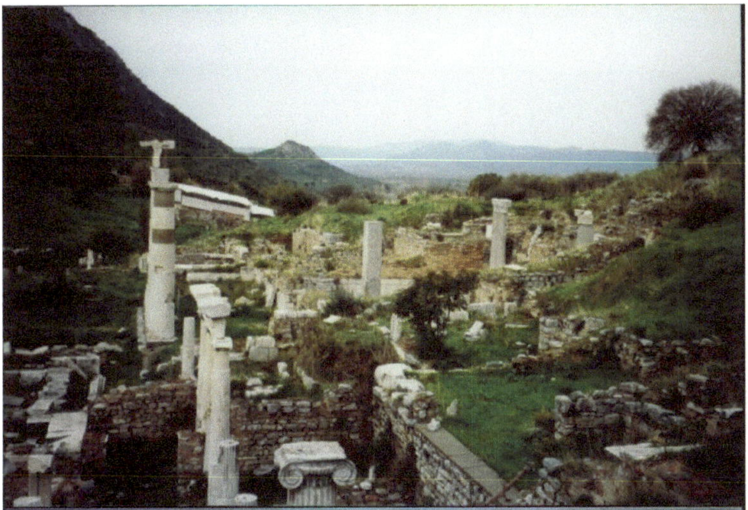

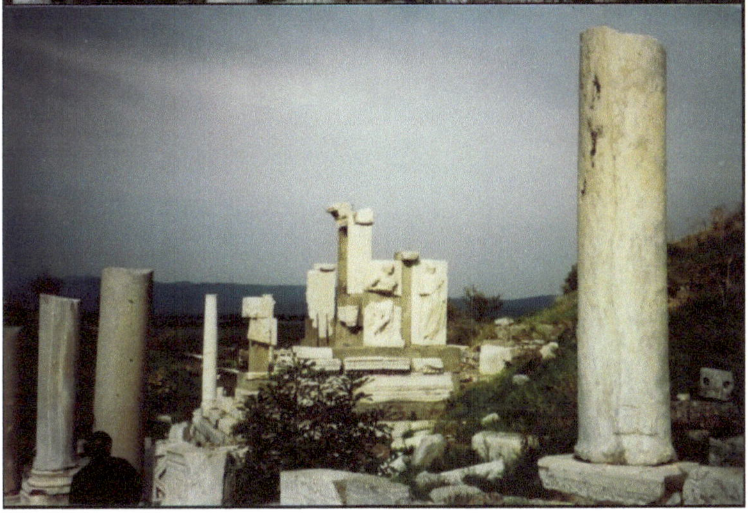

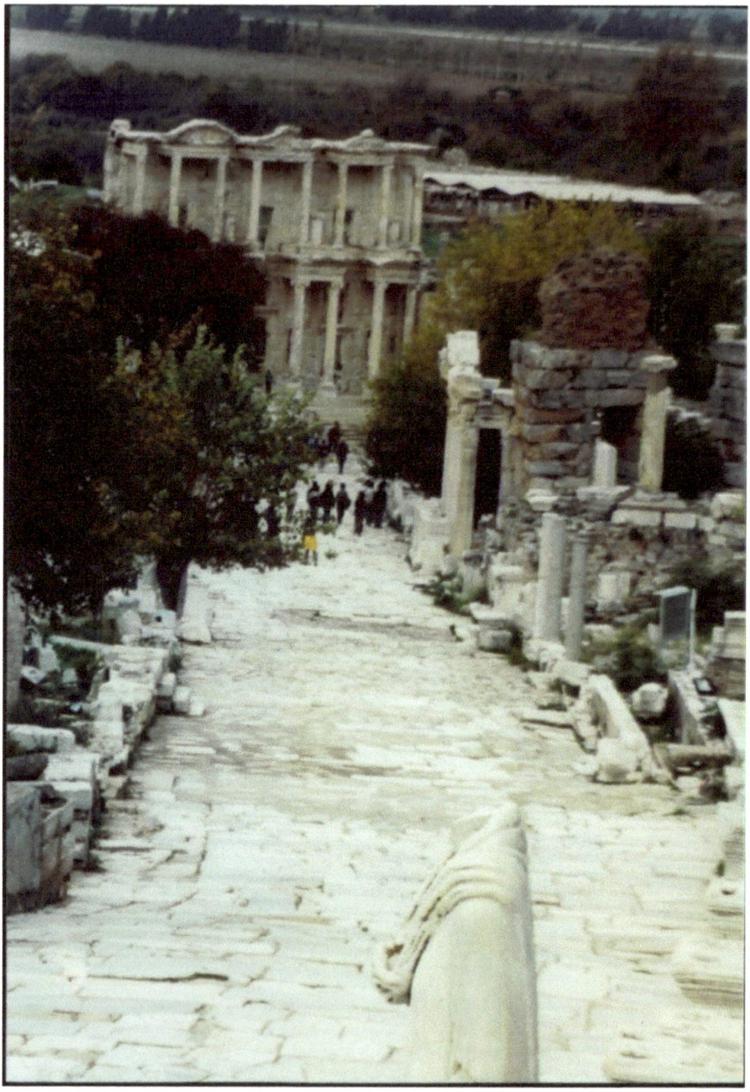

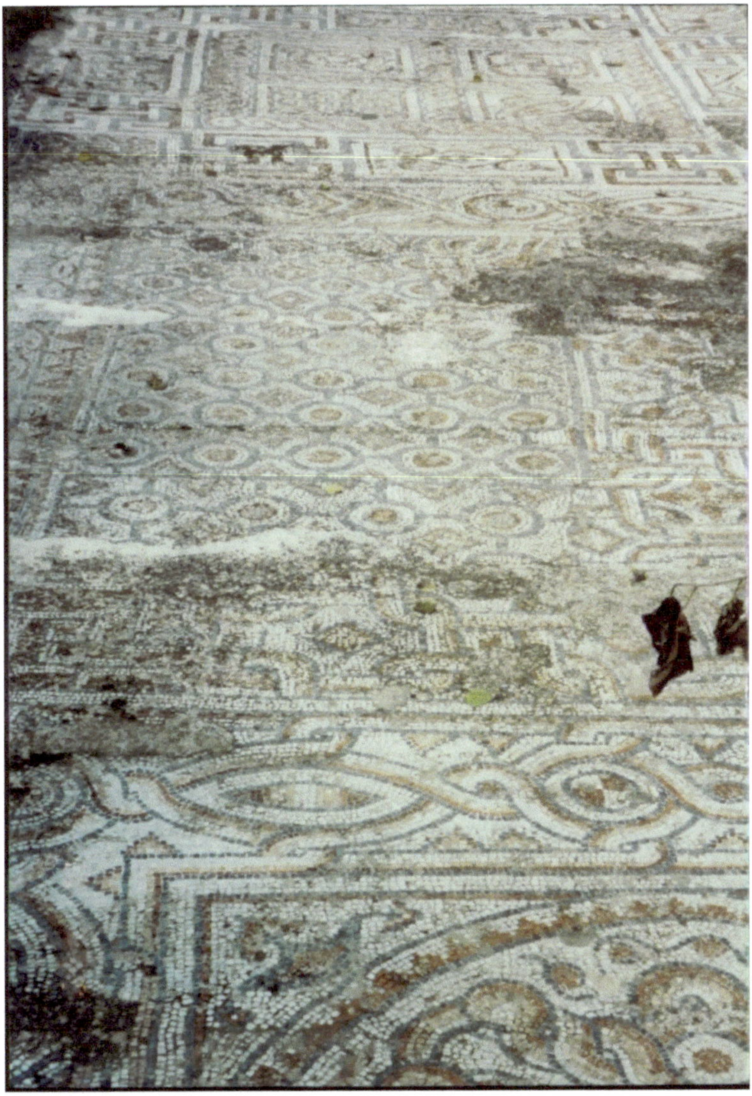

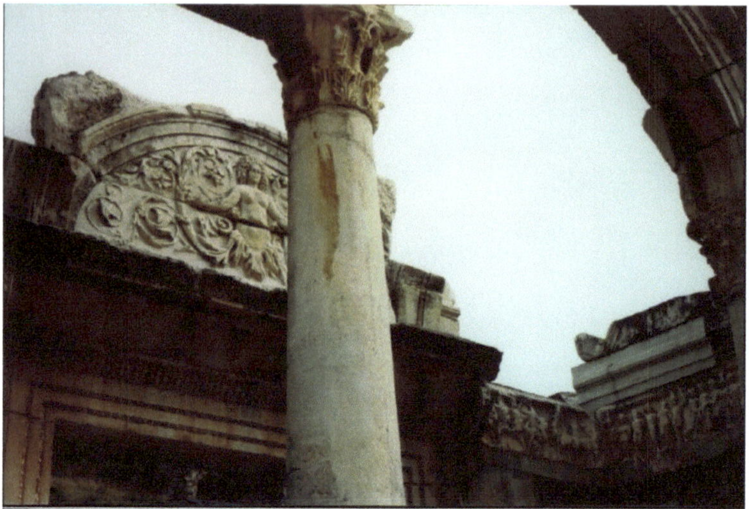

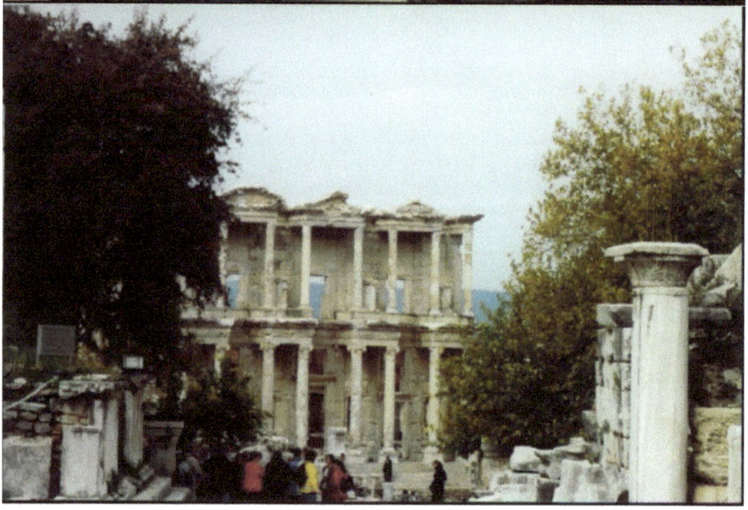

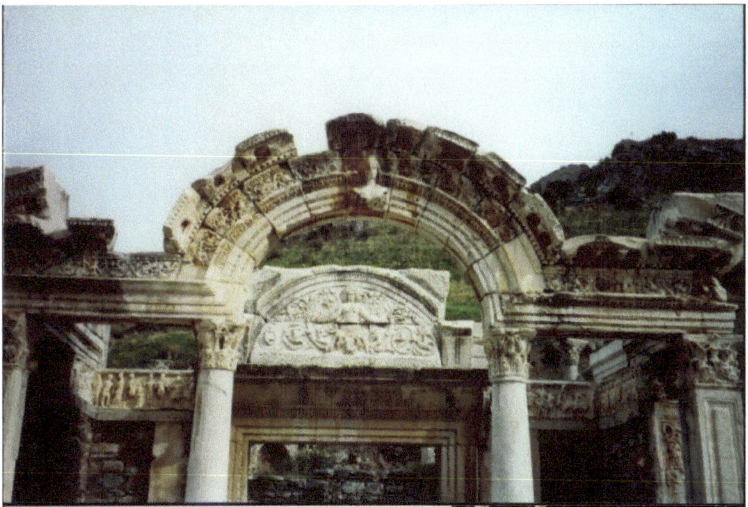
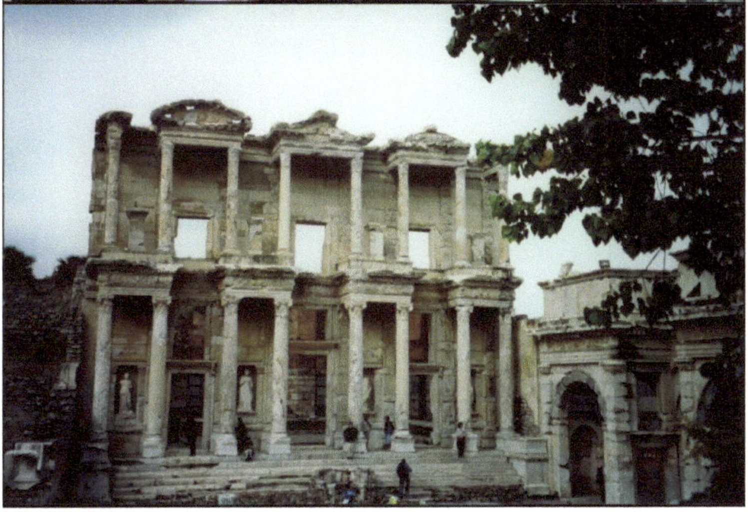

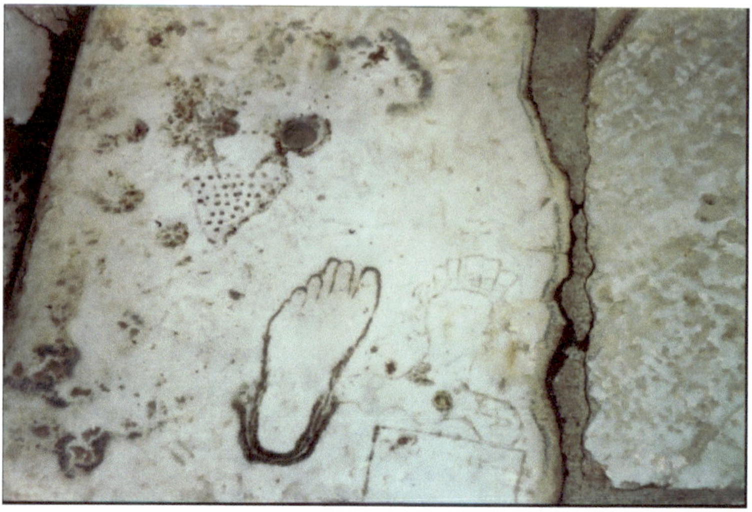

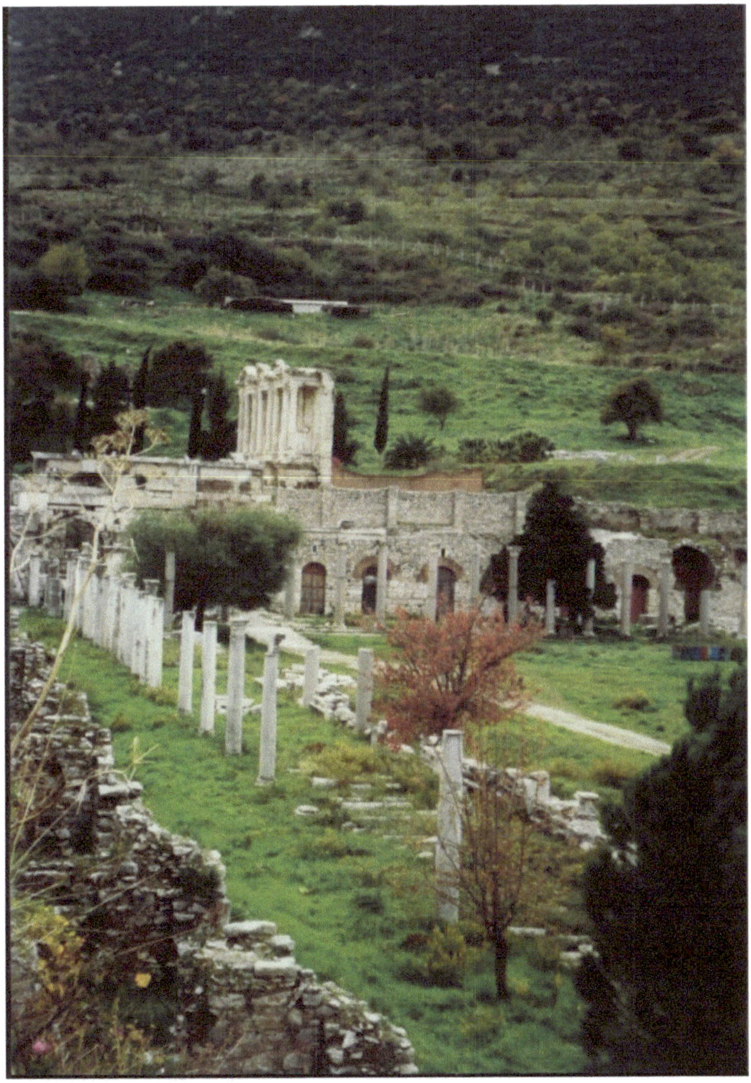

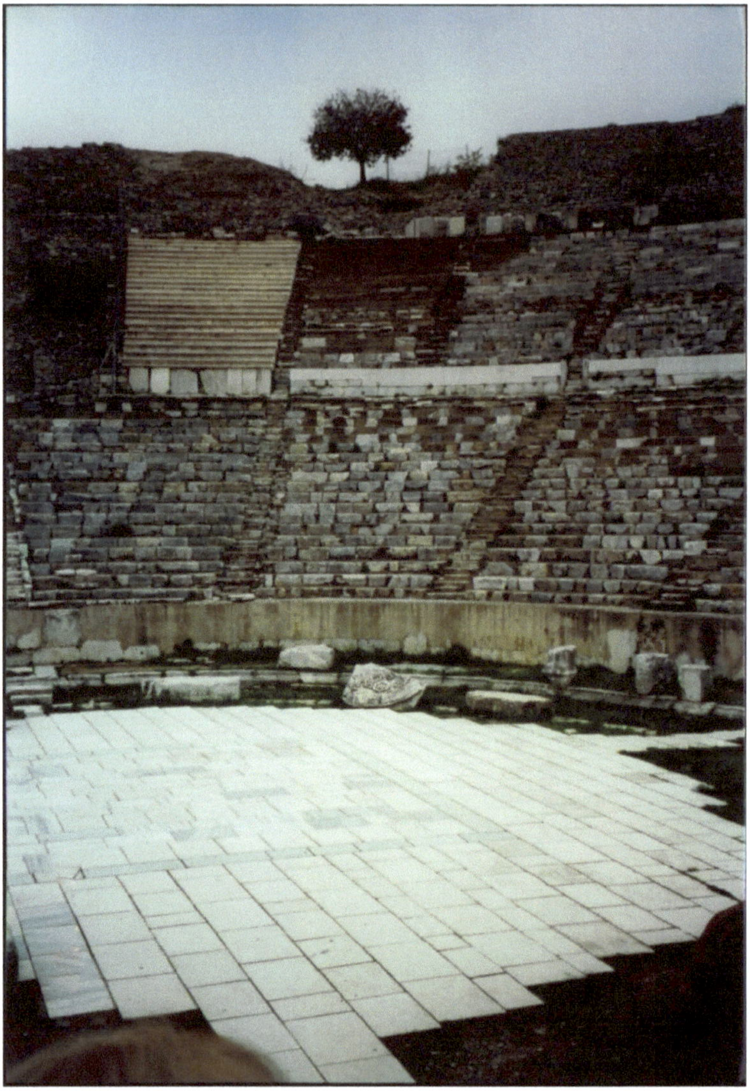

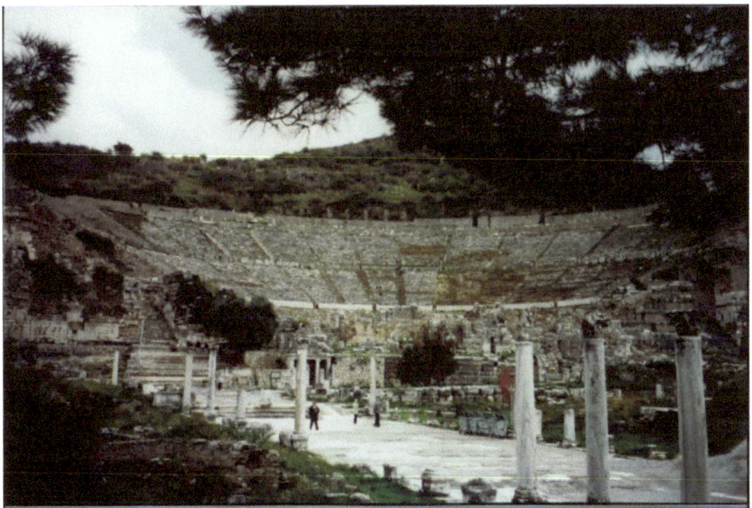

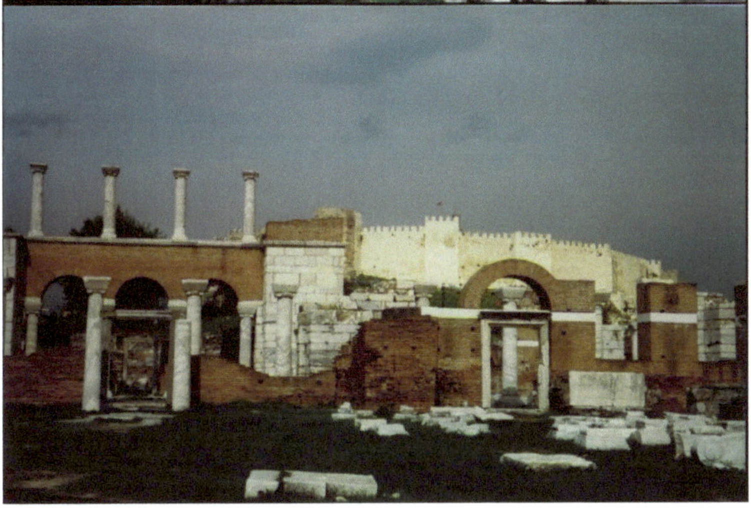

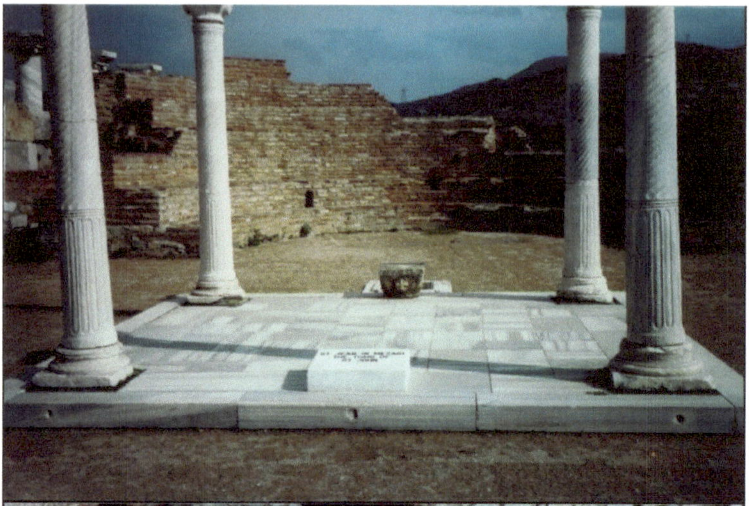

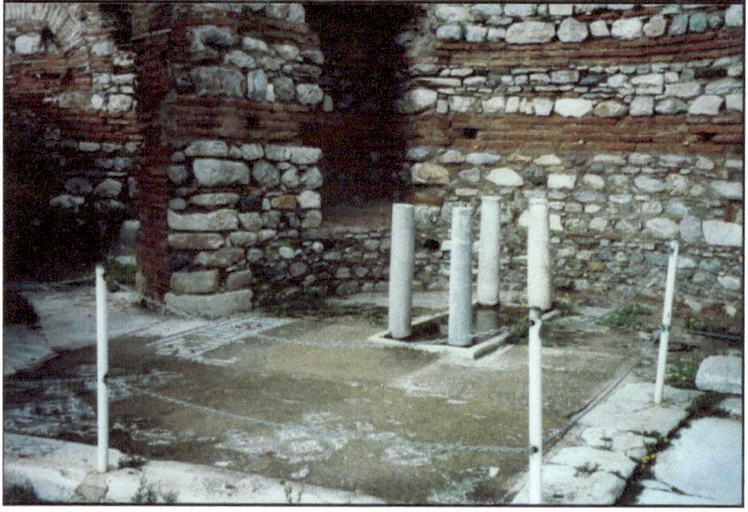

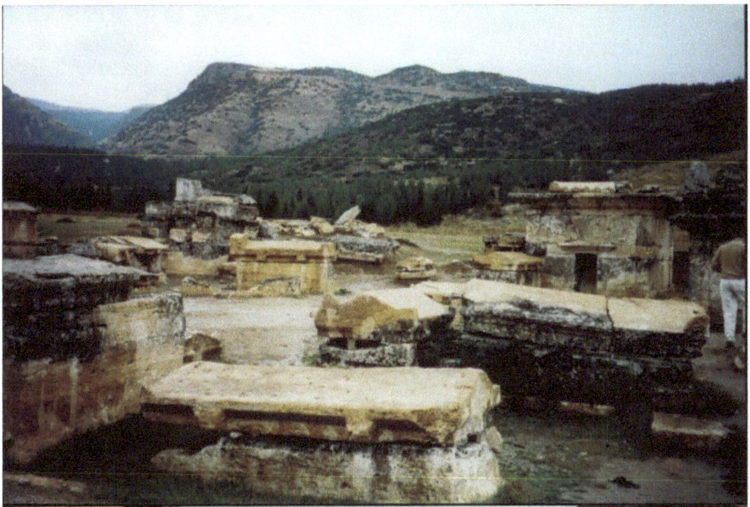

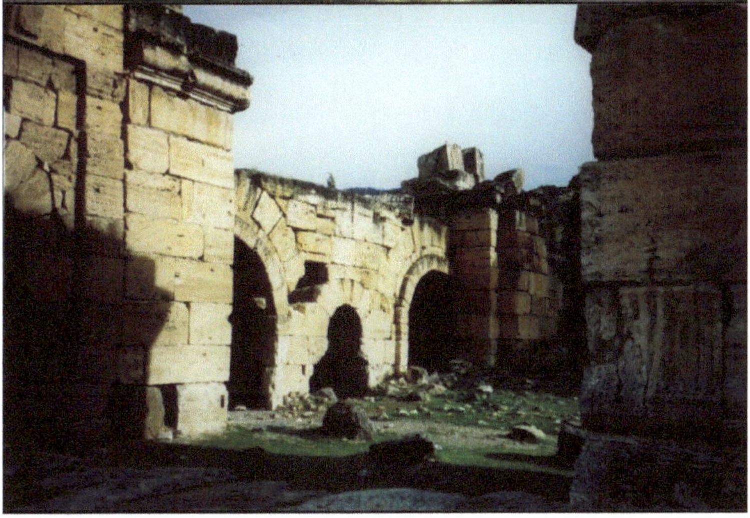

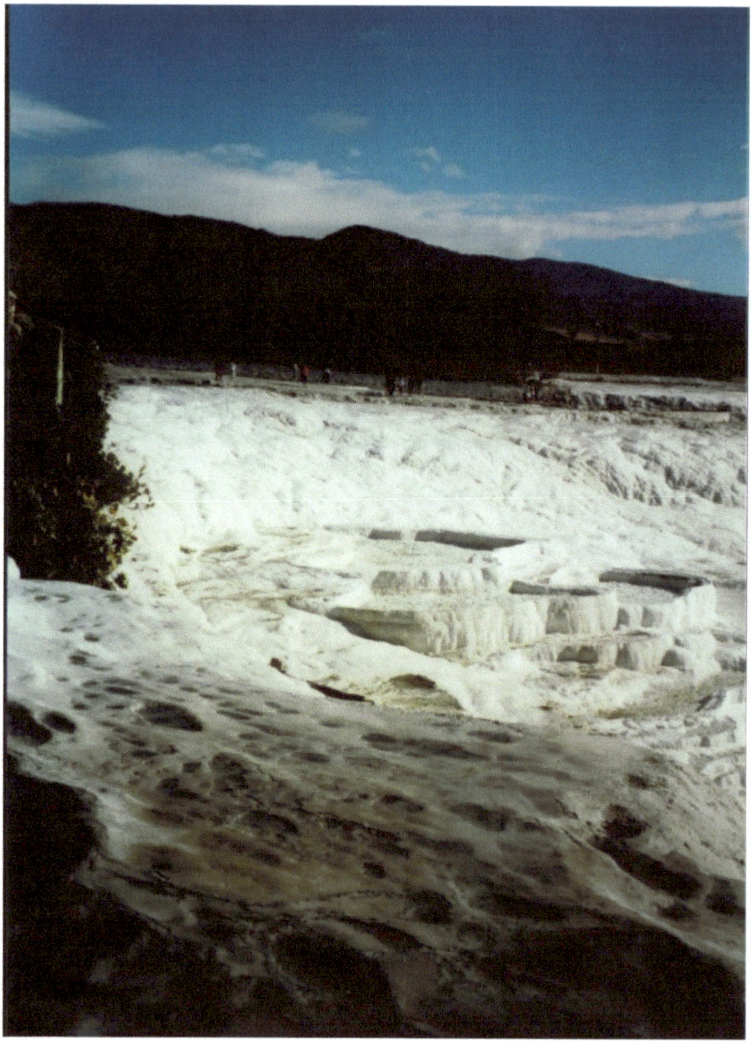

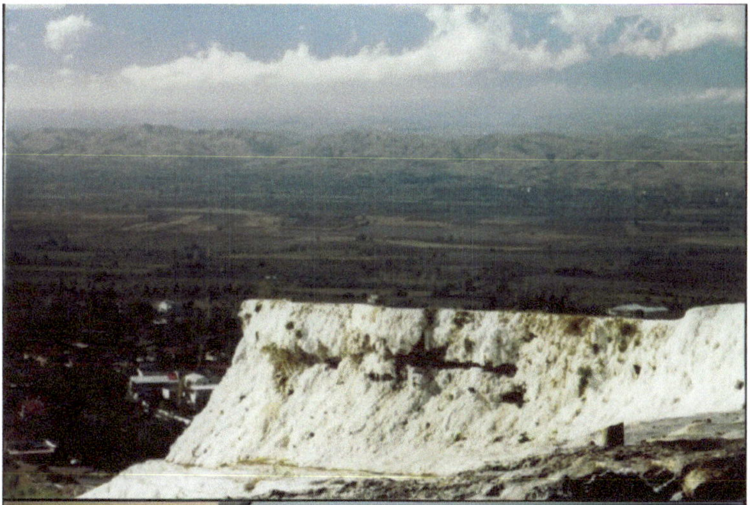

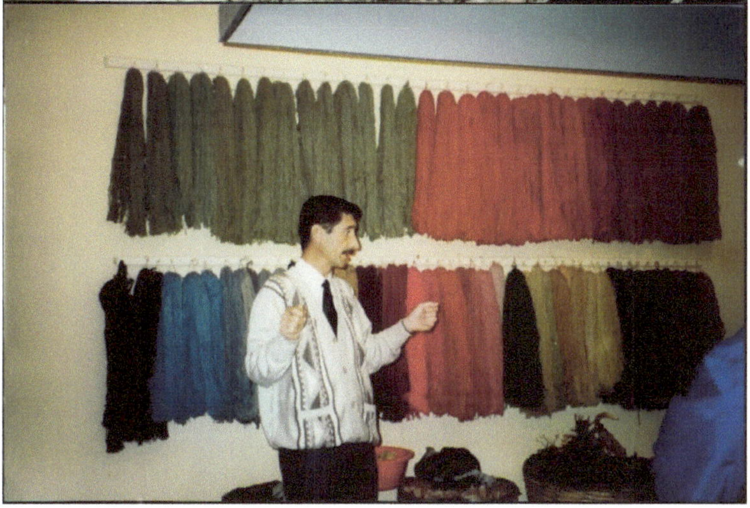

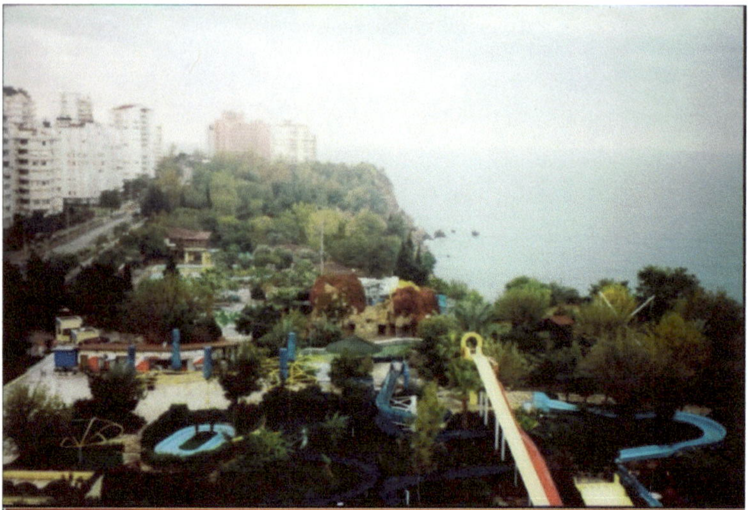
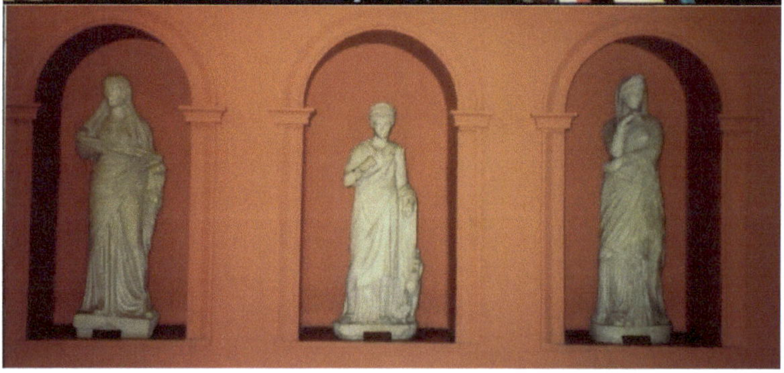

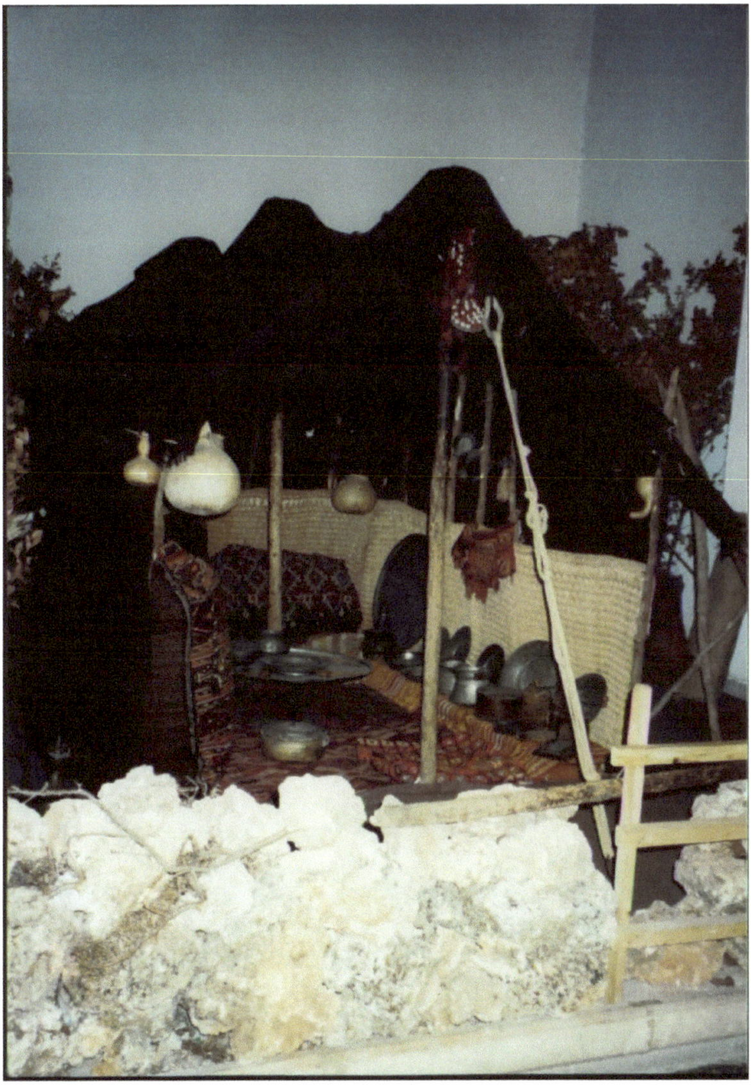

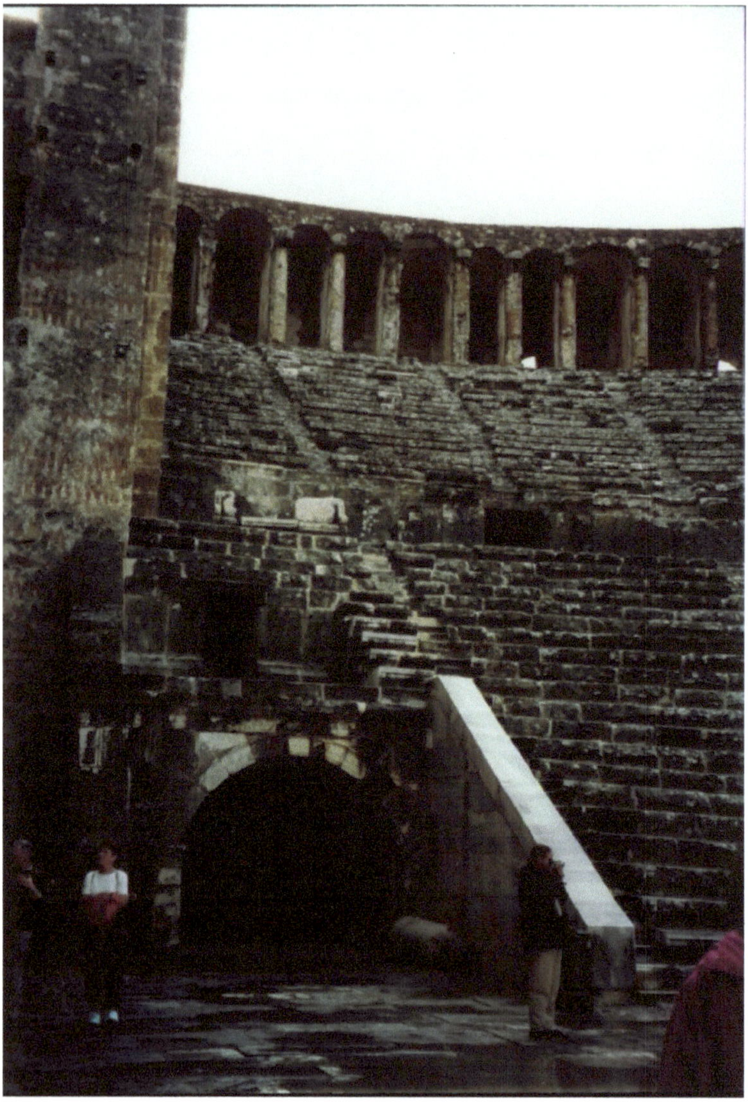

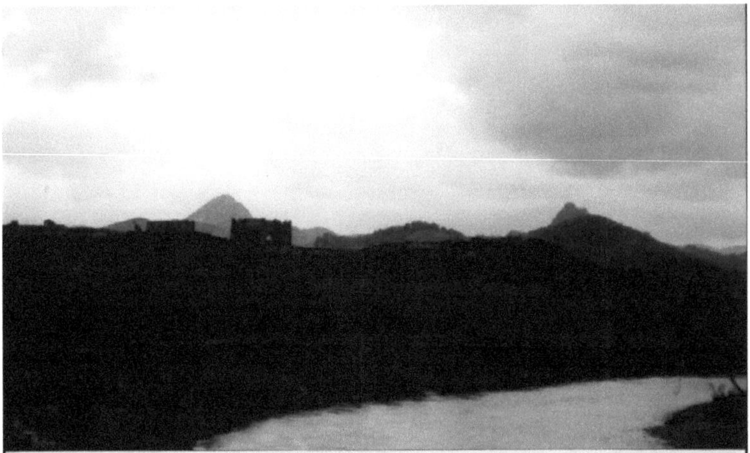

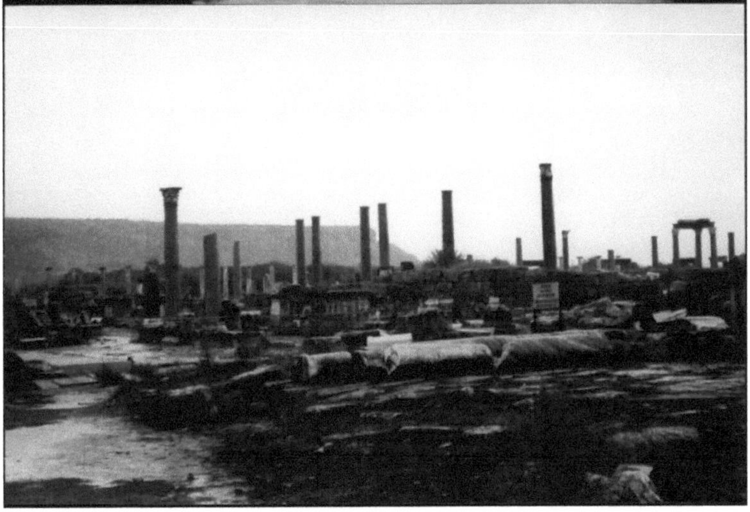

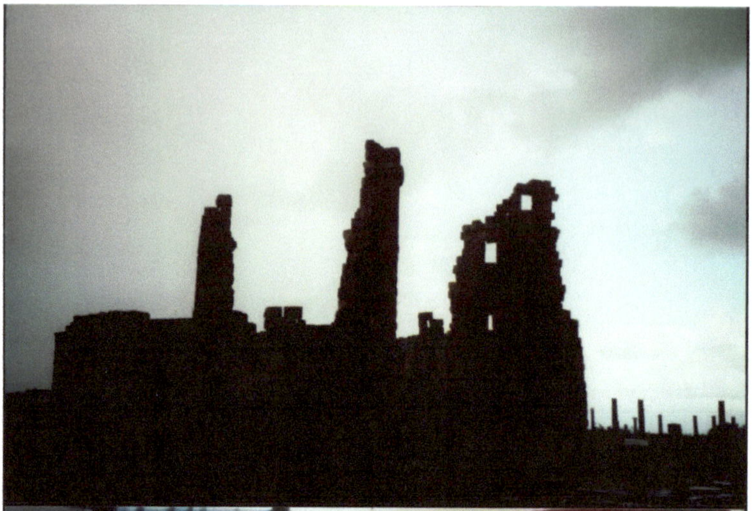

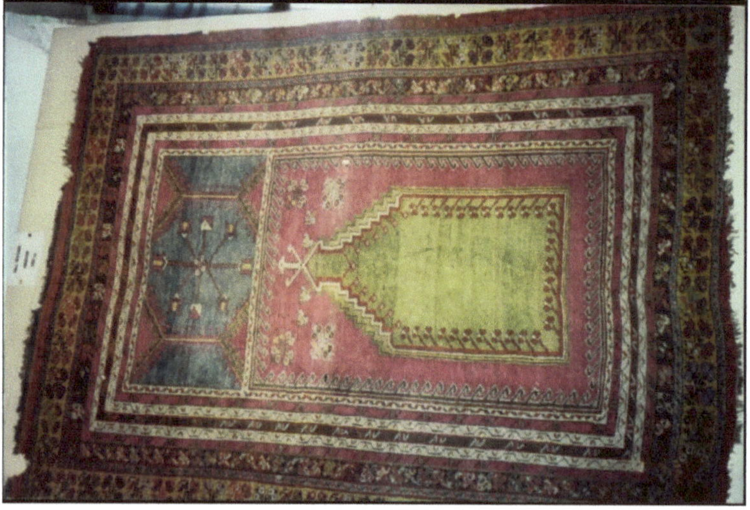

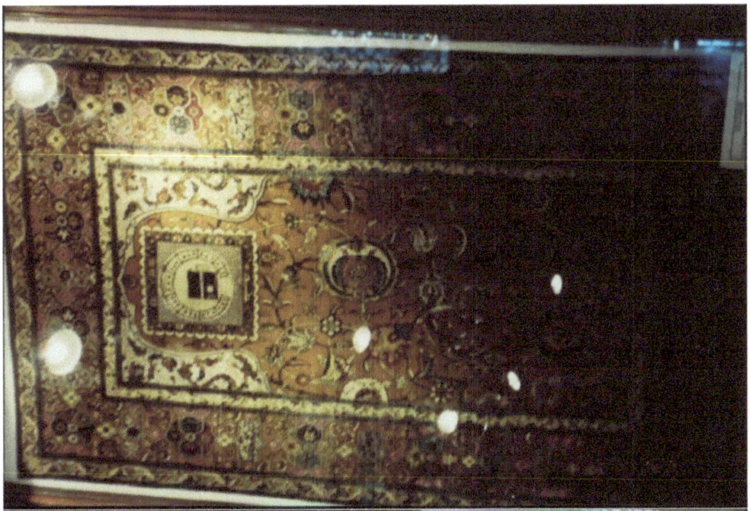

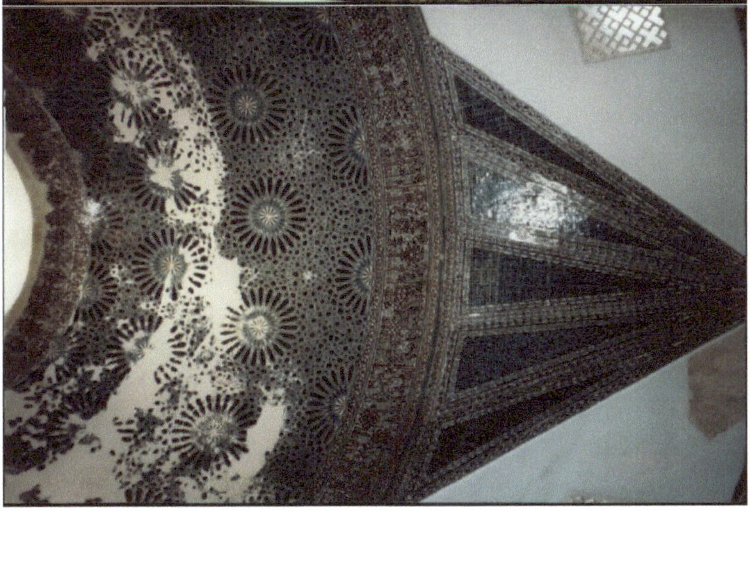

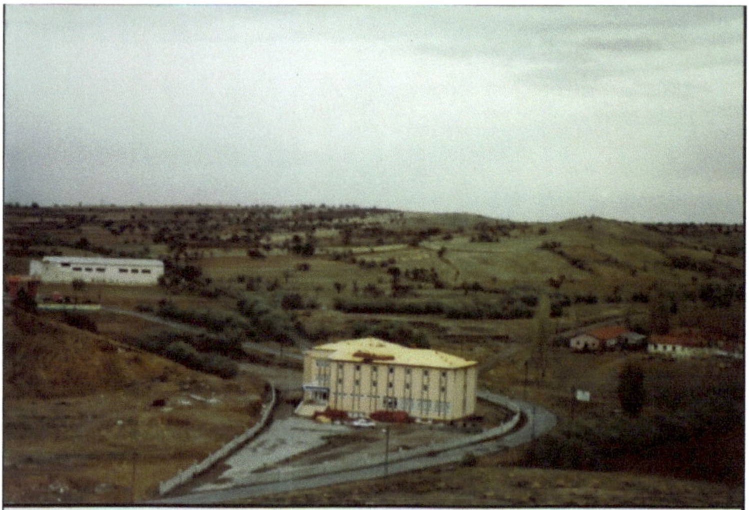

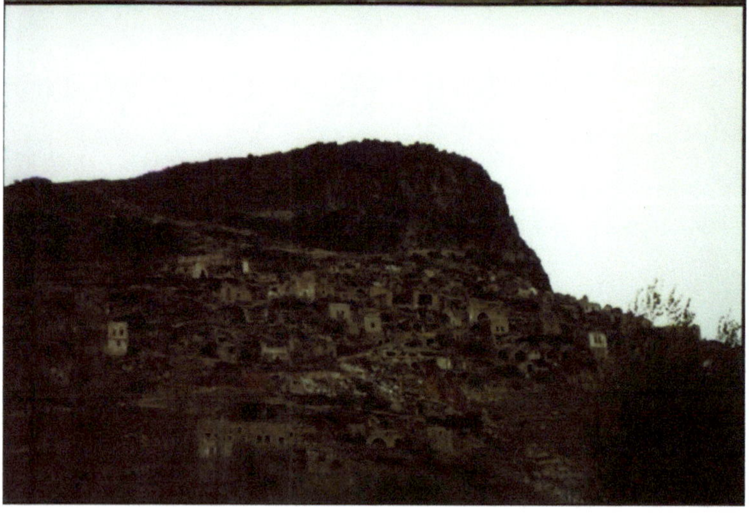

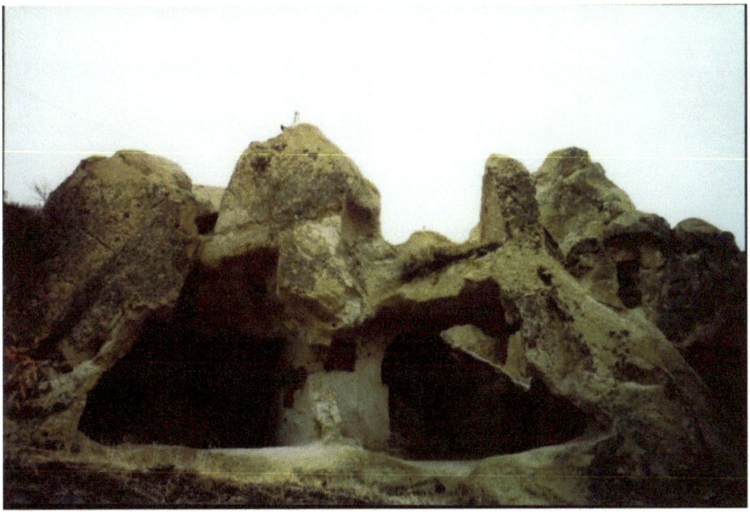

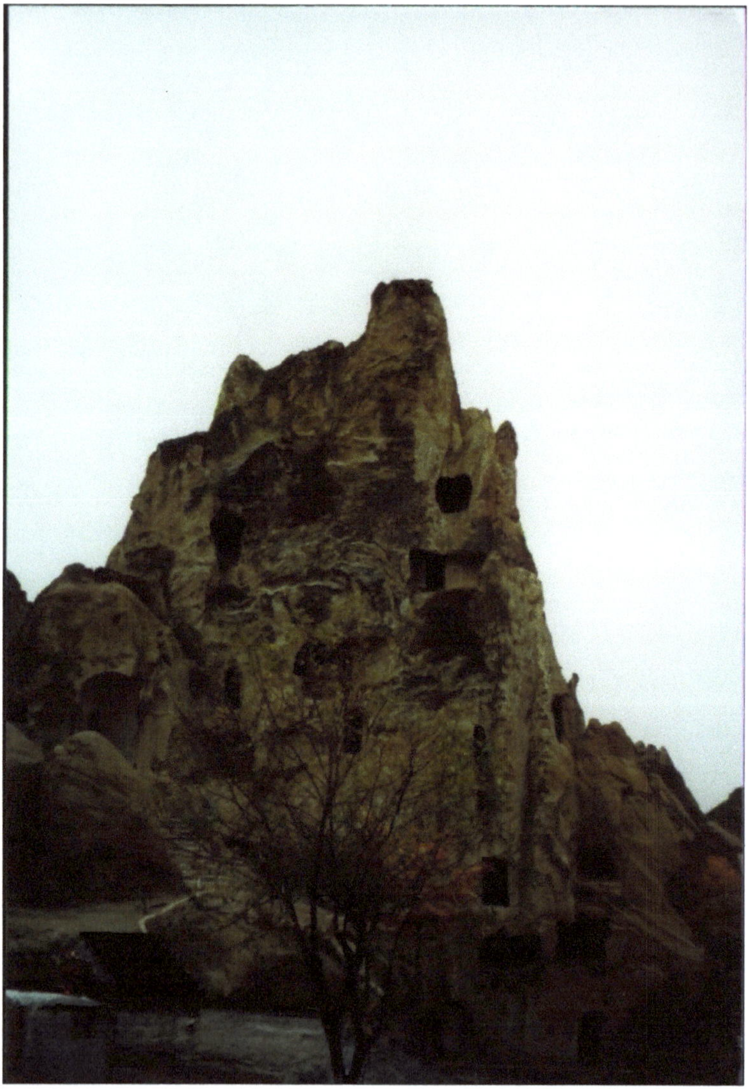

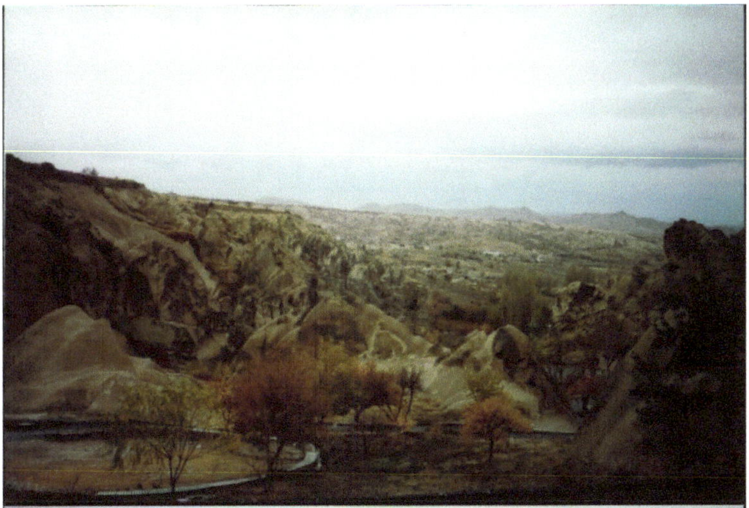

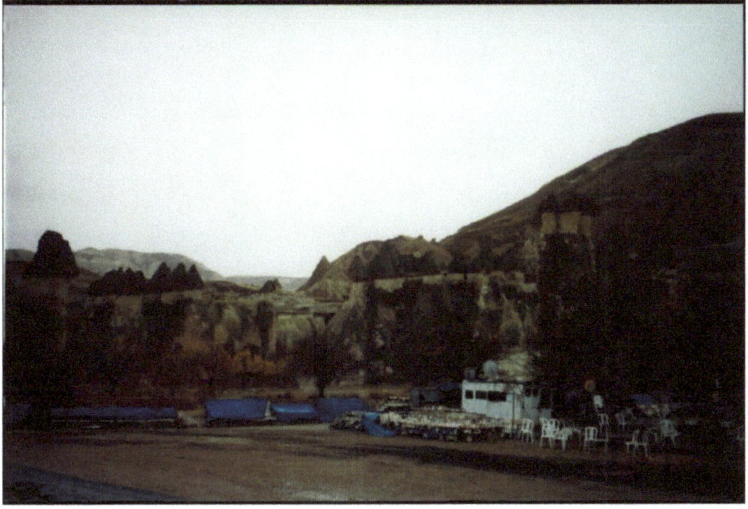

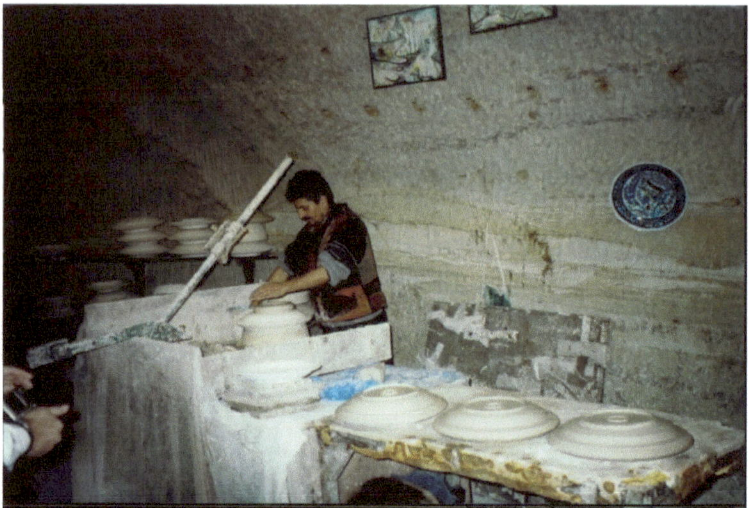

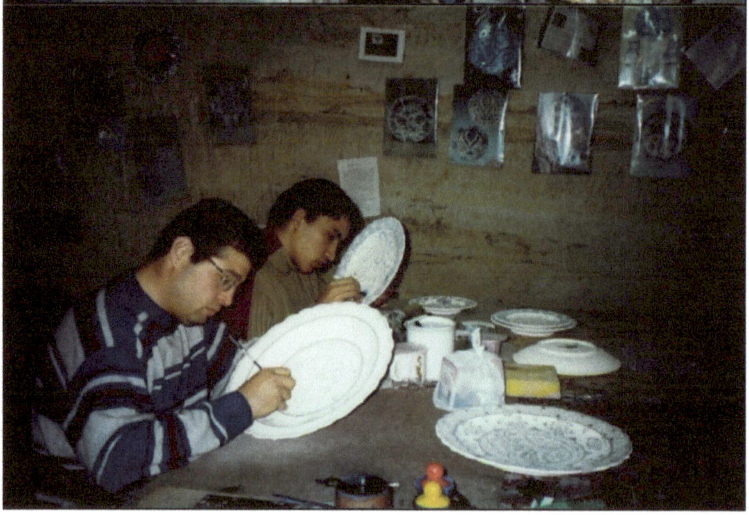

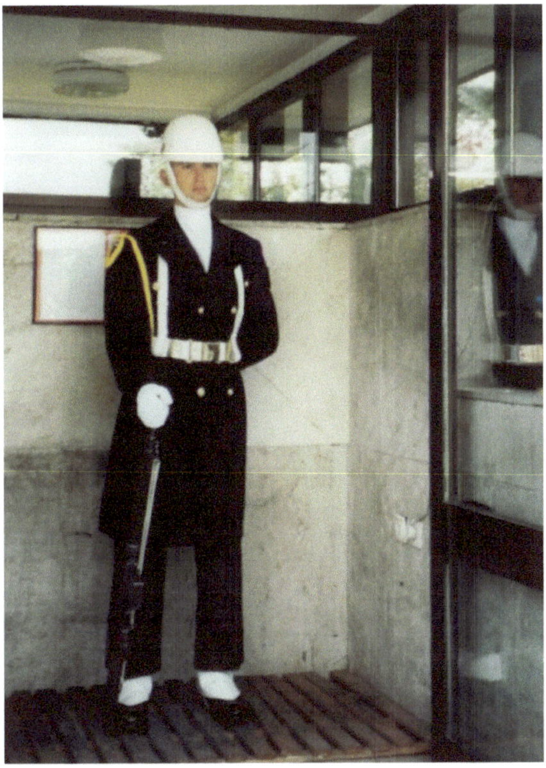

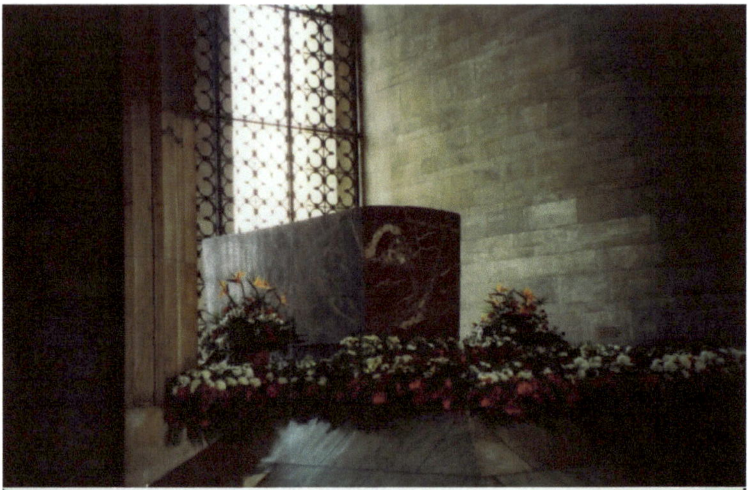

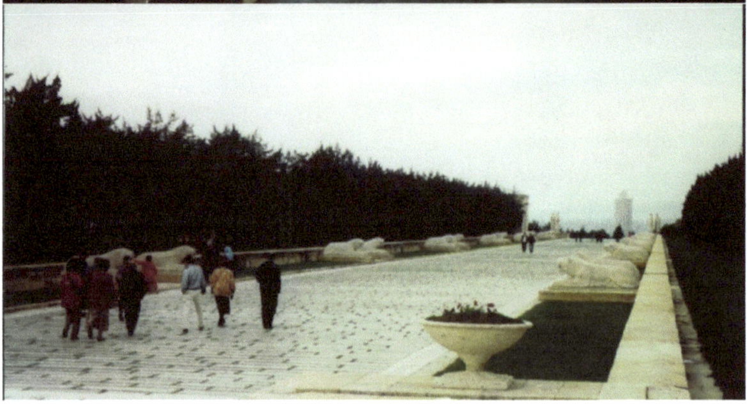

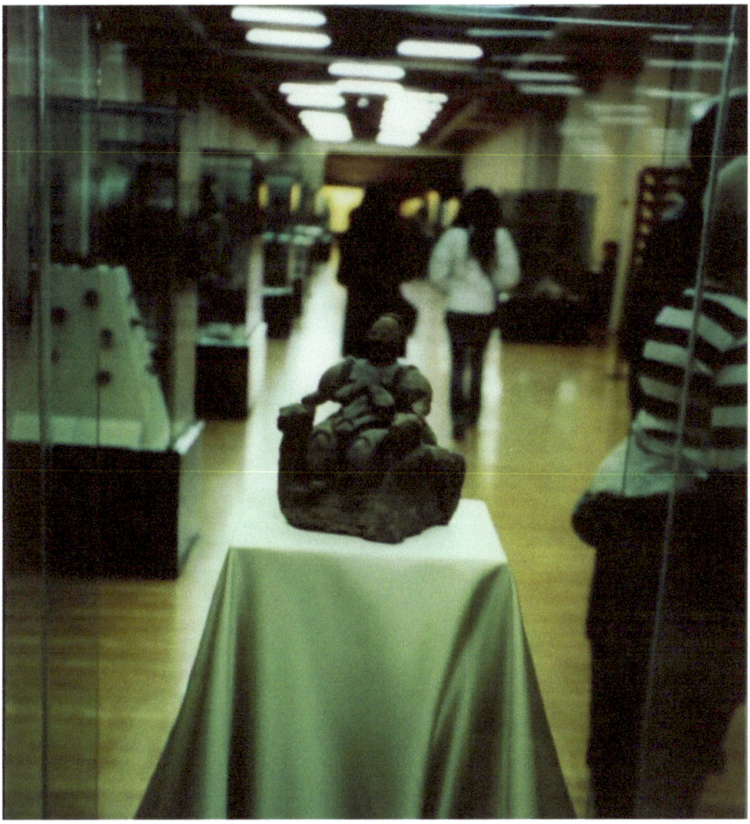

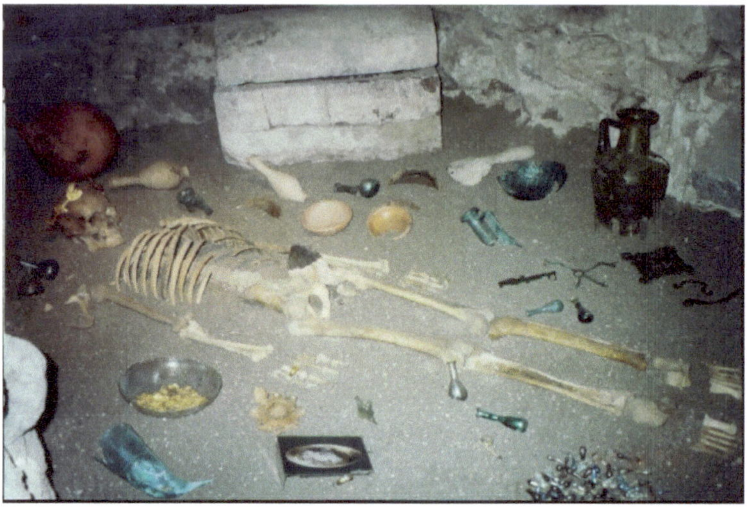

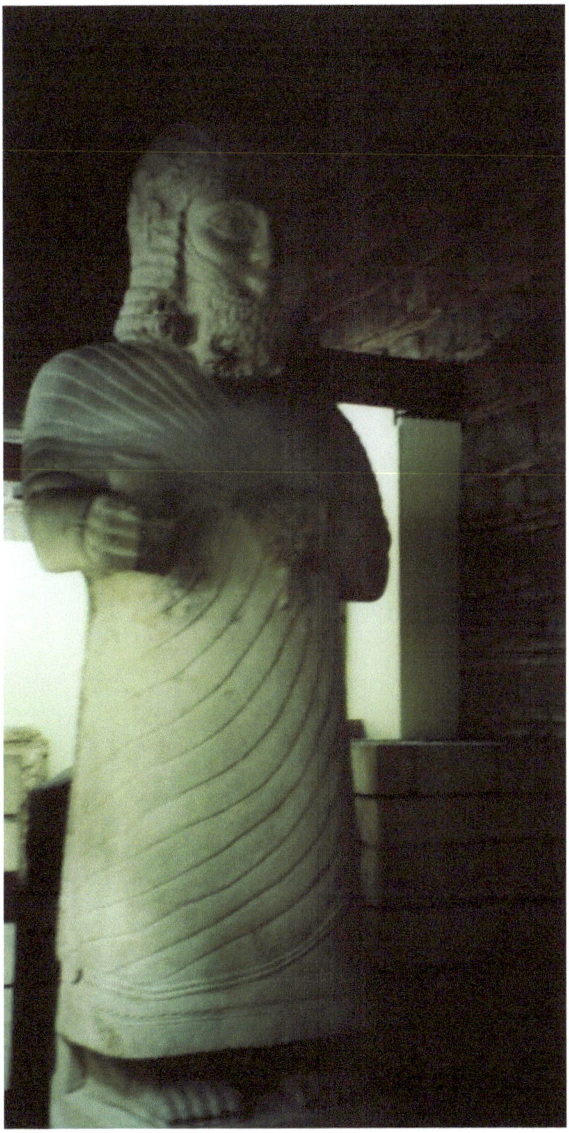

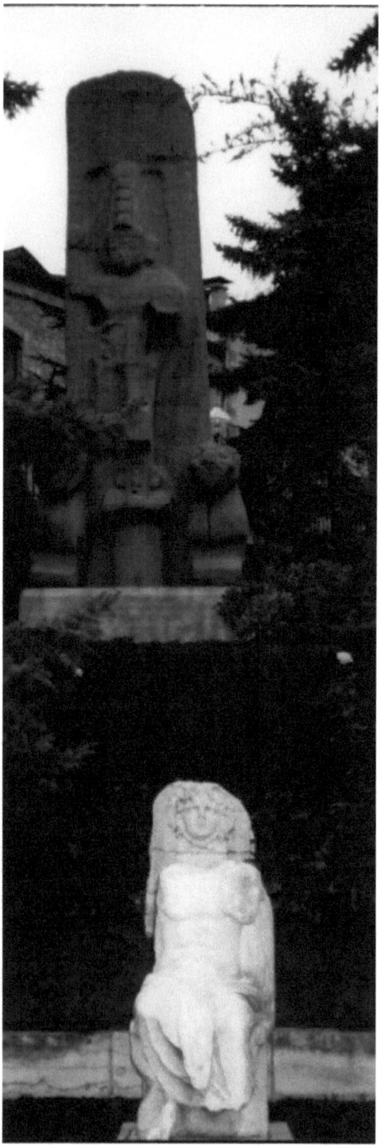

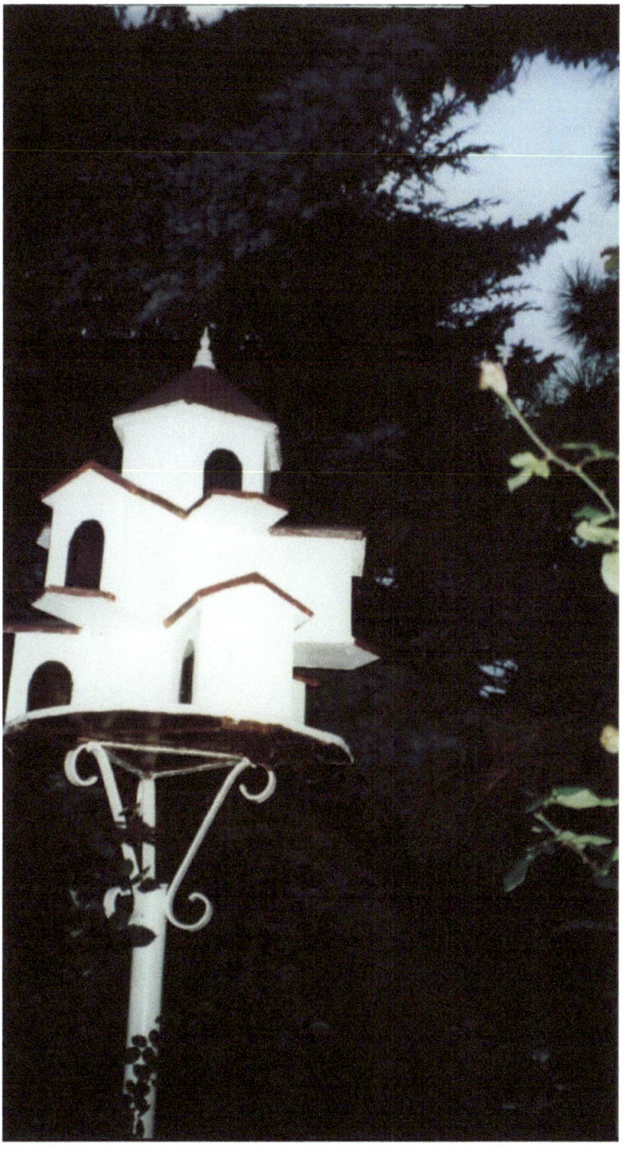

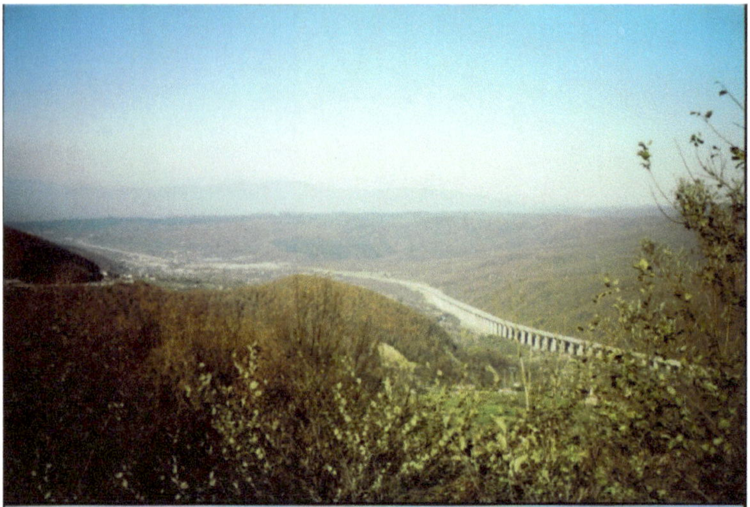

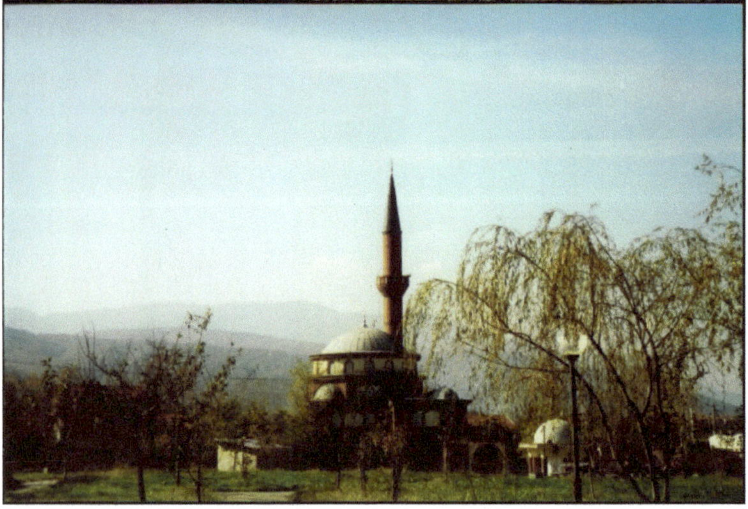

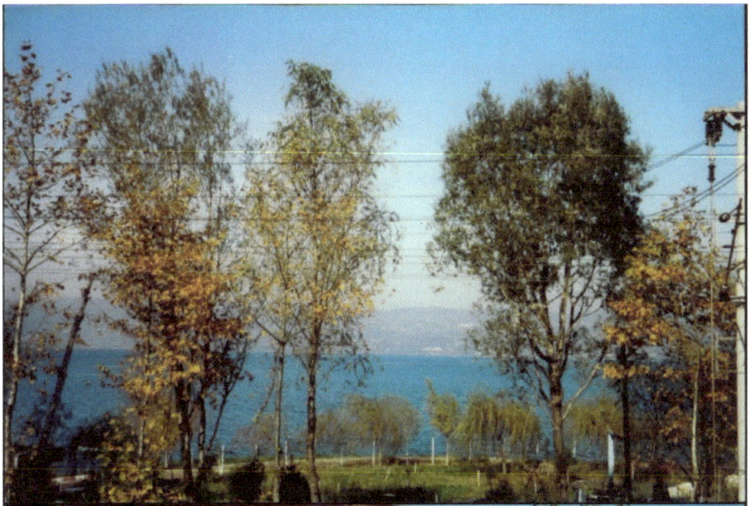

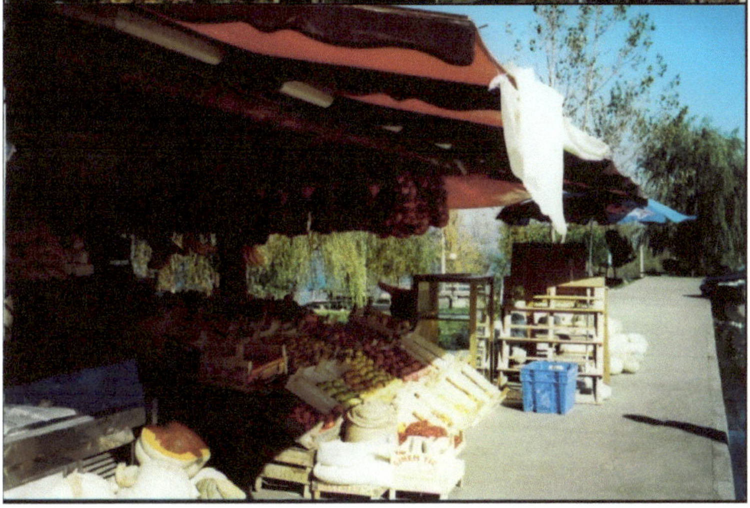

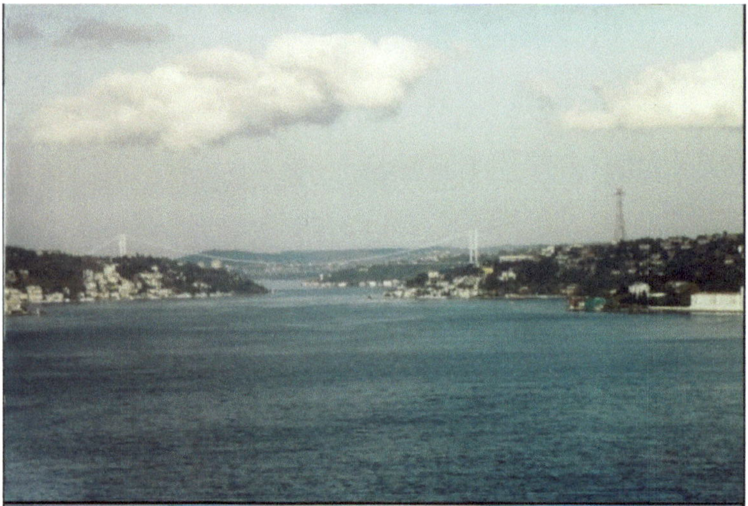

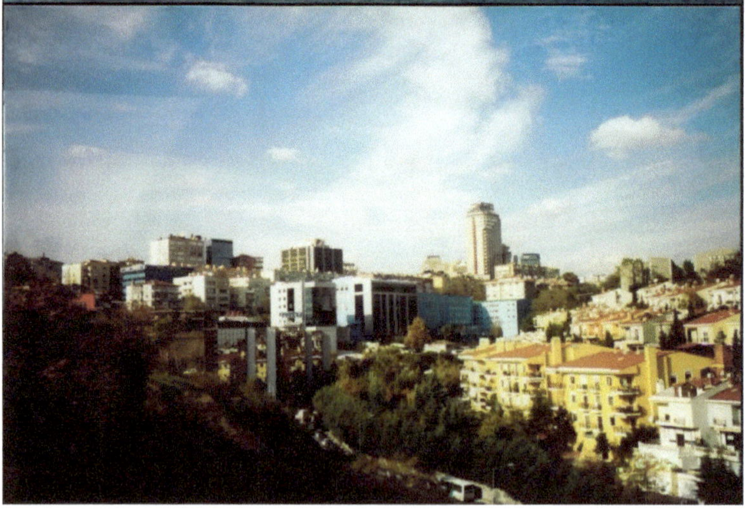

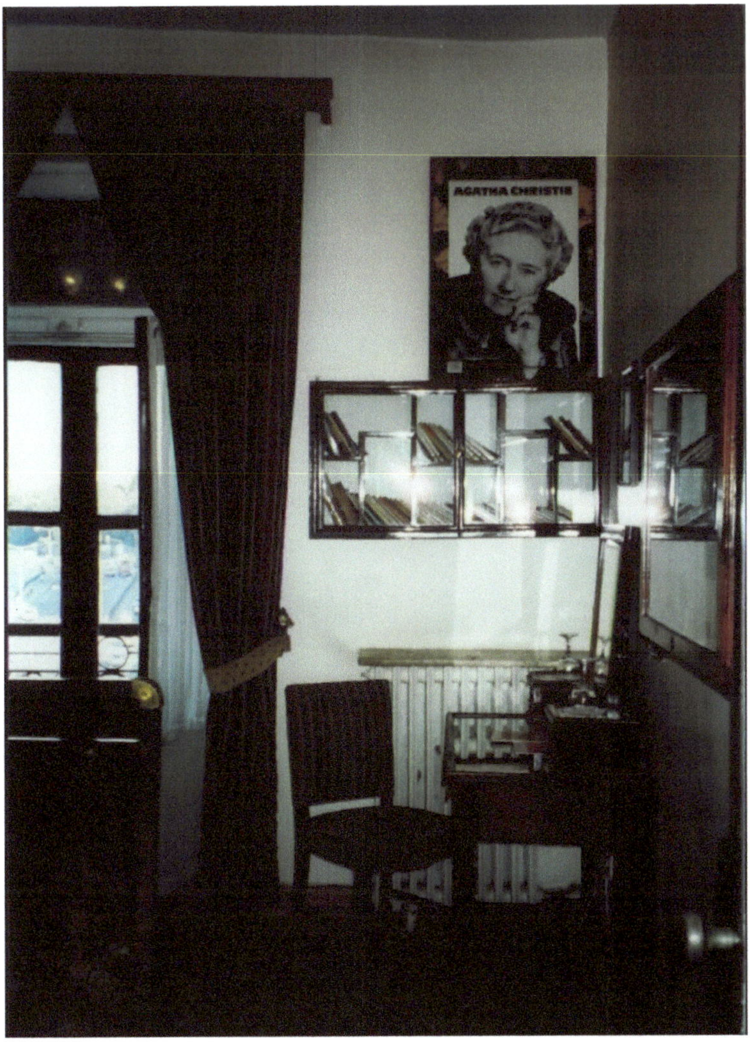
AGATHA CHRISTIE

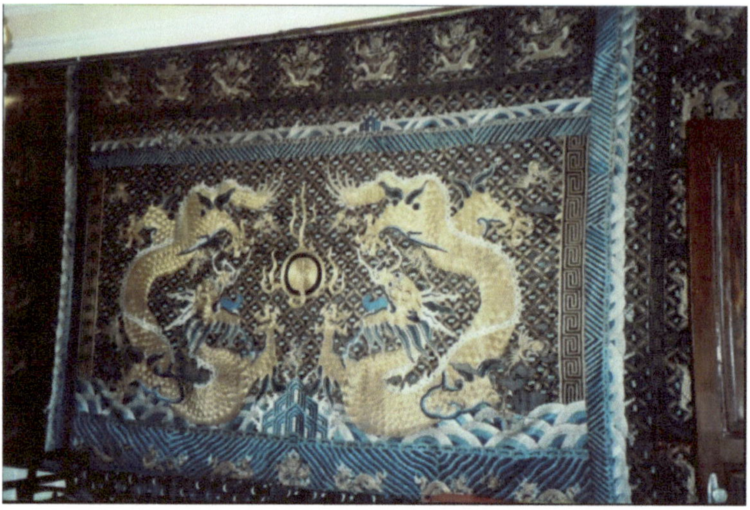

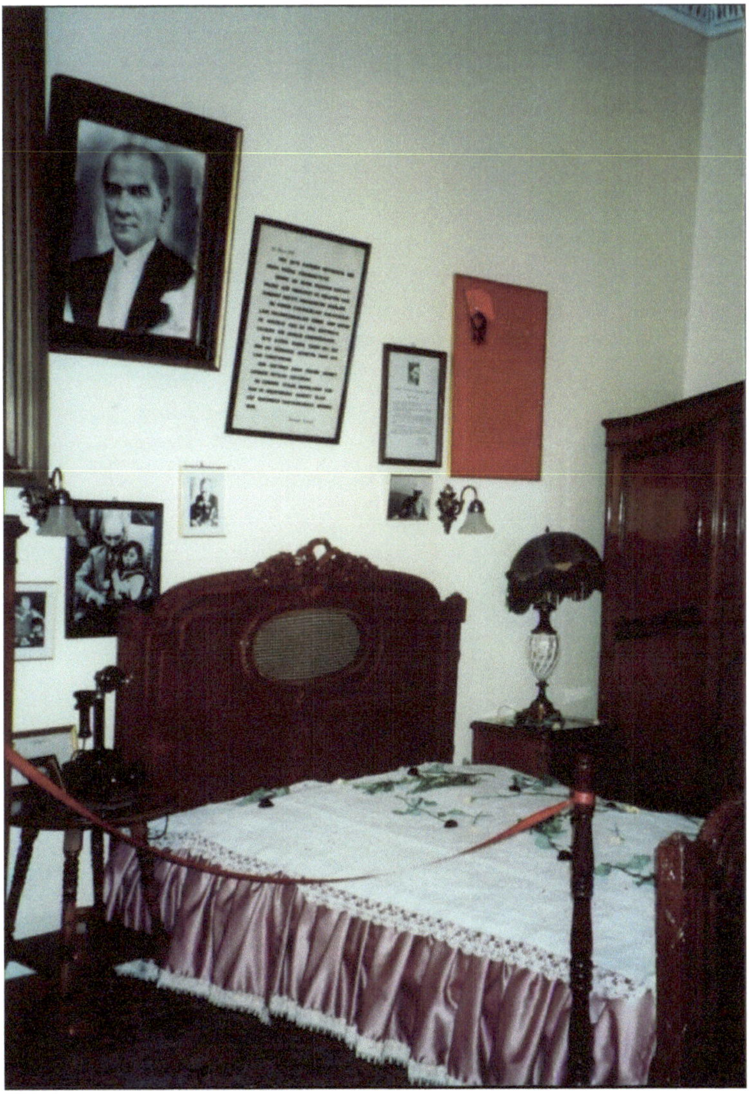

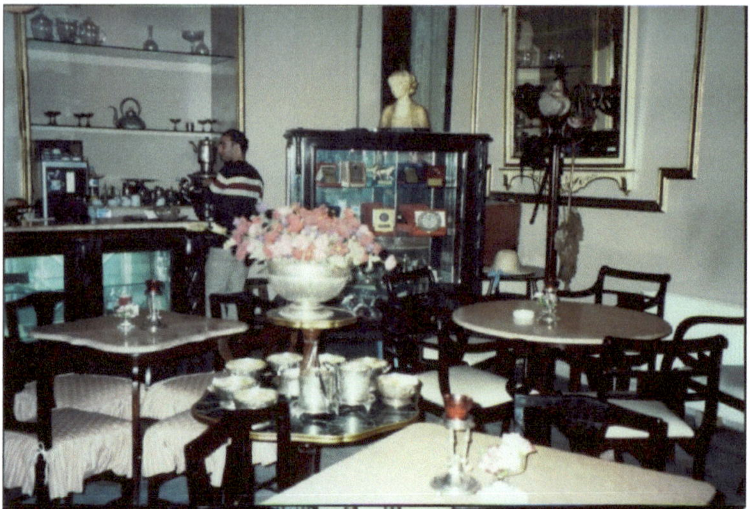

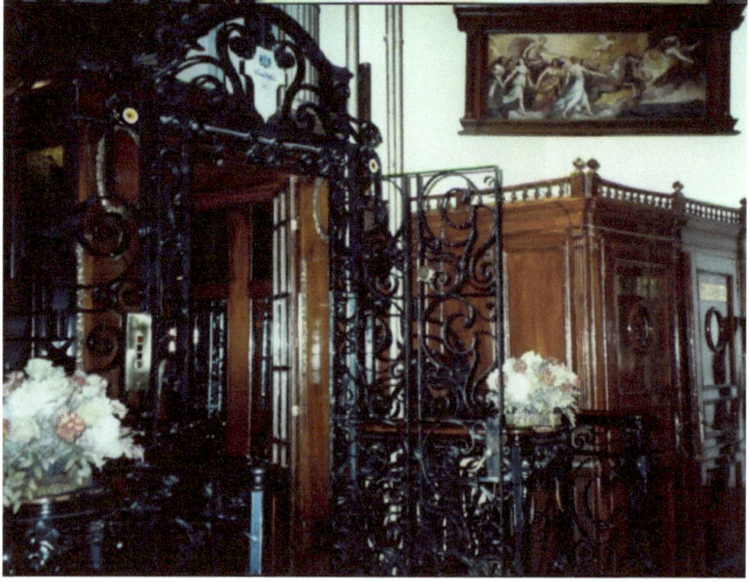

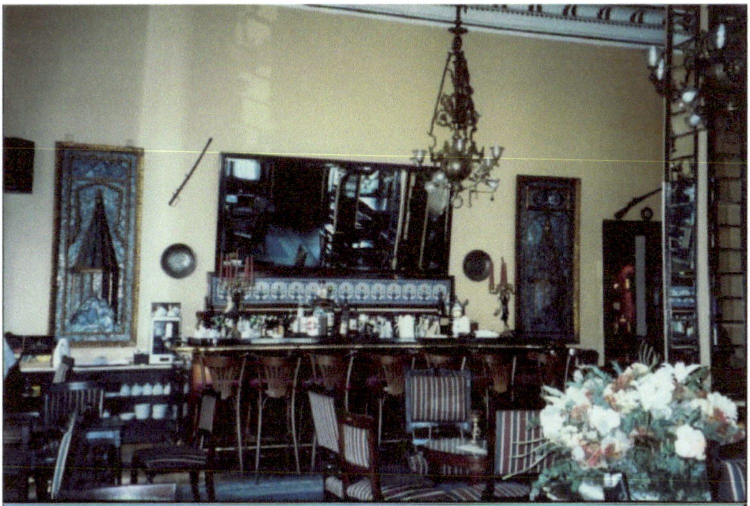

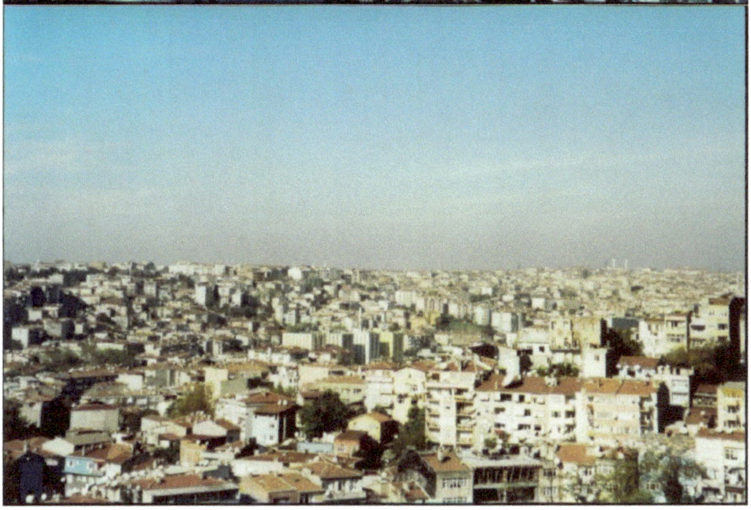

www.ingramcontent.com/pod-product-compliance
Lightning Source LLC
Chambersburg PA
CBHW040902180526
45159CB00001B/495
9781514300688